Let'em Play

What Parents, Coaches & Kids Need to Know about Youth Baseball

Dr. Jack H. Llewellyn, Ph.D.

LONGSTREET PRESS

Atlanta

Published by
LONGSTREET PRESS, INC.
2140 Newmarket Parkway
Suite 122
Marietta, GA 30067

Printed in the United States of America

1st printing 2001

Library of Congress Catalog Card Number: 00-111980

ISBN: 1-56352-648-4

Jacket and book design by Burtch Bennett Hunter
Cover photograph by Burtch Bennett Hunter

Contents

Interviews

To all the parents and volunteer coaches who spend
countless hours creating a positive experience
for young people,

and

To the youngsters I have coached for helping me
understand the challenges and excitement of
being a young baseball player.

Introduction

Why play youth baseball? That's the key question for all young athletes, their parents, and their coaches to consider. Why are athletes motivated to participate in baseball? Why do parents encourage youngsters to play? Why do coaches volunteer to work with youngsters on the baseball fields every weekend? If the answer is – as it should be – *to have fun*, then why do 75 percent of kids drop out of baseball by age 13? If the baseball environment is as positive as we would like to think, then why do parents assault umpires, or threaten kids for poor performance? Why do coaches go to bizarre and frightening extremes to win games? Where is the satisfaction in going 12-0 and having most of your players quit?

No doubt ugly scenes and disturbing incidents have been part of youth baseball since the game began. But the problem has become epidemic. Every spring and summer the sports pages and even the "Life" sections of major newspapers are filled with stories documenting assaults by parents on each other, parents on coaches, coaches on coaches, and even parents on kids or coaches on kids. The following quick review of some of the incidents I personally have witnessed during my more than 40 years in baseball will perhaps help parents and coaches understand why I have undertaken this project.

◉ Two fathers were hospitalized and subsequently arrested for assaulting each other during a T-ball game for five-year-olds when one kid tripped and fell over another kid. The kids were fine; the fathers were not.

◉ A baseball park for 12-year-olds hired a policeman to stand between the home and visitor parent bleachers because so many fights had taken place during games while the kids continued to play.

⦿ One of my young players made an error during a game. His father took him home after the game and had the child stand against the house while his father hit baseballs at him.

⦿ A parent sued the league because his son did not make the All-Star team.

⦿ A parent shot an umpire in the hip after a close call at home plate.

⦿ After a game between 10-year-olds, a grand-mother got out of her car and hit the umpire on the head with a water bottle as he walked past her car.

⦿ At one game in particular, parents constantly yelled obscenities at both umpires and players for no apparent reason.

⦿ A coach picked up a player and physically threw

the kid over the fence when the child started crying after striking out. The coach was also the
youngster's father.

● Two years ago, a coach shot a parent who ques-
tioned his son's lack of playing time.

● The coach of a team of 12-year-olds had his pitcher purposely hit batters on the opposing team, for
intimidation and to teach the kids to be "tough."

● A coach had kids do 15 push-ups after they took
a called third strike.

Obviously, this abbreviated list represents the kind
of thing that should never happen, but that seems to
be happening with increasing frequency. Such incidents are completely deplorable and unacceptable.

Unfortunately, the typical response from some
of the larger youth baseball organizations – that,
overall, the number of such incidents remains
insignificant – is equally unacceptable. If one
child in a million is abused verbally or physically
in youth baseball on a given day, it may seem

unimportant – unless that one child is your child. My point is simply this: One is too many! Let's go to work now to make sure that youth baseball is enjoyable – and safe – for our children. If baseball is organized and taught properly by coaches and supported in the appropriate spirit by parents, then youngsters gain experiences they cannot get in another environment. Baseball is not the savior of children. Rather, it is one vehicle for developing skills that will help them mature both socially and physically. It's also a lot of fun.

Looking back through interviews I've conducted over the past 20 years makes it painfully obvious that these appalling episodes now constitute a serious problem. What's to be done?

Parents and coaches need to think about how to provide a fun, motivating environment for kids. Eliminating parents from the baseball fields is certainly not an acceptable solution. Parents belong there and kids want them there. We just need a better understanding of what's appropriate in the baseball environment. And certainly, volunteer coaches are to be admired for giving their time in the evenings and on weekends to teach kids. Yet we have to do a significantly better job in training coaches in regard to acceptable teaching techniques and behavior. Our governing assumption is that everyone involved in youth baseball agrees upon what is best for the child – i.e., to learn basic skills and to have a fun experience.

Youth baseball was organized to be a pastime, an entertaining activity, a game. And games are supposed to be fun. As kids get older, the game obviously becomes more significant in terms of competition and incentives for achievement. That places the burden on us, as adults, to adhere to some guidelines, to monitor our own behavior, to control our own emotions. Above all, we must constantly remind ourselves that our athletes should play because they want to play, because they enjoy it, and because they learn admirable skills and receive positive feedback for their efforts.

The purpose of this book, then, is to provide parents, coaches, and athletes with information that will help them enjoy a fun, exciting, competitive, and fulfilling baseball experience year after year. Kids need to understand why they play baseball. Parents need to understand why they encourage kids to play and understand their respective roles in the baseball environment. Coaches need to understand why they coach, a pretty significant question to explore. All three groups must know going into baseball what they want to have accomplished when they make the decision to walk away from the game. To walk away after we have fulfilled our aspirations is wonderful. To quit because we've had a miserable experience is terribly unfortunate.

Part 1
Tips for Parents

First, let me make it clear that I enthusiastically support parents' participation in youth baseball. Probably 95 percent of parents do a great job. Unfortunately, the other 5 percent get the media attention. During recent meetings that I attended, the "quick fix" was to eliminate parents from the field. In fact, programs in two states have made national news by instituting "quiet weekends," during which parents were either prohibited from attending games, or allowed to attend but not allowed to make a sound. If the purpose of these quiet weekends was to call attention to the issues, they certainly did the job. But as an actual, long-term remedy, they are totally off base. For the benefit of the youngsters, and their parents, such a solution is unacceptable.

It goes without saying that parents are the most important people in their children's lives. In a recent survey, we found overwhelmingly that the players want their parents to watch them play, to watch them practice, and then also to practice with them at home.

According to current statistics, both parents work in 51 percent of two-parent homes. Perhaps there is some connection to the excesses in parental behavior at youth baseball games and the lack of quality time with children elsewhere. Maybe parents try too hard to use a one- to two-hour time slot to make a significant impact on their child's life. Obviously, you cannot pack a full day's interaction into two hours. Realistically, what you can give in that brief period at the park can be expressed in two words: *support* and *encouragement.* Time, or lack of it, is obviously an issue. But used wisely, this short block of time can be very productive.

It is so discouraging to go to a baseball complex and see the dwindling number of parents attending games as the kids get older. Parental participation is great in T-ball and up to the eight- and nine-year-old levels. After that, however, the number of parents attending games diminishes progressively until spectators number close to zero for the late teen years. But the fact is, these teenage years are when youngsters desperately need parental support. A missed game is a missed opportunity for you to be there for your child – to be *with* your child – and these missed opportunities never return.

Remember: *fun* is the goal of youth baseball. Two factors help your child reach that goal: first, learning how to play; and, second, knowing you are going to be there to support him and to assure him that he has a "winning" experience.

The following tips for making a memorable contribution to your youngster's youth baseball career have been gleaned from many years of experience with youth baseball programs.

I hope that you will not only read this list now but also review it during the course of the baseball season. It will help you be all that you can be as a parent in your local youth baseball program.

I. SELECT THE RIGHT PROGRAM

Perhaps the first question to ask is why a youth baseball program? Did your child ask to sign up, or did you suggest it? Has your child had a chance to play other sports? Sometimes parents are more anxious to get their kids in a youth baseball program than the kids themselves are.

However, if your child does show a genuine interest in baseball, then you have an obligation to select a program that will best meet your child's needs. Too many programs are selected only because of convenience; i.e., close enough for your child to bike to the park, or with enough car-pooling available so that parents can *not go* if something else comes up on practice day. This is not to say that convenience is not an issue; it is and should be, but not the determining factor.

Here are some factors you *should* consider:

◉ Your child's age and ability

◉ The coach's ability and qualifications

◉ Involvement of parents

◉ Fair participation for every player

◉ Winning kept in proper perspective

◉ Individual attention for each child

A number of other criteria might be considered, but these should be at the top of your list. I'll elaborate briefly on the first three.

Your child's age is without question the most critical concern. If your child is going into T-ball – five or six years old – then above all the program must be FUN. Obviously, the program should teach skills, but the child must be eager to go to practice and to games.

Many T-ball programs use the "T" for hitting, but others use "coach-pitch," in which case you may be asking your child to learn too many skills at the same time: to swing the bat correctly, to track a moving ball, and to make contact at the perfect time. For the beginner, this might not be much fun. There should be some progression in learning. I suggest picking a program that uses the "T" and does not progress to coach-pitch until the kid can hit the ball off the "T" consistently.

You should also be concerned with the coach's abilities and the program's evaluation process. Does the program monitor coaches? I am familiar with one large program in which coaches may be disciplined by suspension for a year or longer or by demotion to assistant coach. On the other hand, another program I know of refuses to discipline coaches because of a "coach shortage." And yet another program, which several years ago won the Little League World Series, tolerates any coach who wins. But when you look at long-term participation of youngsters in these programs, you'll conclude that any argument against careful monitoring and evaluation of coaches is superficial and ignorant.

In fact, one factor you should always consider in selecting the right program is the turnover rate among players. Heavy turnover is likely to signal problems in the program, and these problems may well have to do with the coach.

One thing you can observe yourself is the

coach's teaching methods. We know, for example, that it is very difficult for a youngster, without baseball experience, to learn both catching and throwing at the same time. Kids should be taught to catch first, and to practice catching until they have eliminated all the unnecessary cues. For example, when a child is trying to catch a moving ball, initially he visually attends to everything in the universe that is moving – people, dogs, cars, clouds, etc. Eventually, he will eliminate the cues that have nothing to do with the ball and learn to focus on only the ball. At that point it's time to move on to throwing.

And third, be sure to select a program in which parents are involved – not just as cheerleaders, but in this teaching and learning process. Regarding the example above, the worst situation is to have two five- or six-year-olds throwing and catching with each other. One can't throw and the other can't catch. More generally, though, parent involvement is an integral part of the whole experience and offers a wonderful opportunity for sharing, bonding, and quality time.

For parents, program selection is the toughest

decision to make. And, then, monitoring the program you've selected can be a time-consuming process. But this effort is necessary to ensure that your child has a positive experience in youth baseball.

PAUL O'NEILL

Right Fielder, New York Yankees

- ★ Five World Series Championships
- ★ Five-time All-Star
- ★ AL Batting Champion, 1994
- ★ Only Yankee to hit over .300 six consecutive seasons
- ★ One of only four Yankees to have at least 100 RBIs four consecutive seasons
- ★ Father of three

I started playing baseball when I was about six years old and probably started Little League when I was eight. I had four older brothers who played as well, and my dad coached.

But I was also playing football and basketball. In fact, basketball was my favorite sport throughout high school, and I was recruited by some big schools. I got drafted out of high school, though, and that's when I finally settled on baseball. When I was younger, I pitched, played first base, and played in the outfield. But I was drafted as an outfielder, and that's what I've been ever since.

The most important person in my youth baseball career was definitely my father. He coached our team for several years, but even after that, he never missed a game. In fact, my dad told me from day one, "You will play in the major leagues." That had a huge impact on me, and I never forgot it. But that's probably because I already had such tremendous respect for my dad. He passed away during the 1999 World Series.

Besides my dad, though, I had good coaches throughout youth baseball. They always had a positive attitude, they believed in discipline, and they made sure we played by the rules.

The most important thing I would tell parents is that you cannot and should not force your kids to play. Once they show an interest, though, let them play and encourage them to play. Play with them. Throw the ball around with them. Get them a ball and a bat. What I used to do is, I would throw the ball up, hit it, and then run, and get it and do it again.

But, like I say, I had four older brothers who played, and there was nothing I liked better than walking to the high school and watching them play.

Also, once kids have expressed an interest, parents should help them find the right program, which mainly means finding one with the level of competition that's right for their child. Parents should also learn all they can about the coach, and they should teach themselves everything they can about the game.

What I would remind coaches is that every kid is different, and you have to coach them differently. You have to motivate them differently. A coach also must establish his credibility. The kids need to know that the coach really understands the game. The coach has to have the kids' respect, he has to be the one in charge, and the first step to doing this is showing that you know the game.

No question about it, youth baseball was a great experience for me. I absolutely loved to play. That's what it was all about. I also learned how much fun it is to win, especially since we got to go to the Dairy Queen after we won. But I also learned that no matter how well I played, or any other individual player, it took the *team* to win.

One thing I didn't learn in youth baseball, though, was how to deal with losing. That's because, looking back, it seems like we won just about all the games we played. It wasn't until I got to the minor leagues and played 100-game seasons that I began to understand that you're gonna lose some games. And you have to get over it and get ready to play the next one.

II. TRY TO EVALUATE THE COACH

If possible, you should choose the coach for your child, but this isn't always an option. Most leagues have a regular draft where they "buy" the kids. Sometimes, the best you can do is request that your son be on the team with a friend.

However, some parents opt to become coaches themselves and coach their son's team. That can be the best – or the worst – of worlds for you son. It can work well if you coach your son exactly like you coach the other team members; it's a disaster if your expectations and your coaching focus exclusively on your son. It goes without saying that you must attend equally to all the members of the team. Also, if you take this route, you must also remember to coach your son during practices and games, not on the way to and from practices and games.

Two extreme examples of the "worst world" scenario come to mind. In one instance – cited earlier – a coach threw his son over the fence after a strikeout. Clearly, the coach would not have thrown anyone else's son over the fence – at least not without risking a serious parent confrontation.

The other example is the coach who demanded push-ups after strikeouts. He was also incredibly hard on his own son, the pitcher, whom he often left crying on the pitcher's mound between innings. He also left his wife fuming in the stands.

Assuming you don't coach, you would obviously be more comfortable knowing that all the coaches are qualified. But remember: most of these coaches are parents . . . and volunteers. Most have not had coaching experience or training. Perhaps some of these coaches have taken one of those quick courses consisting of a book, a lecture, and a few video tapes, and concluding with a test and a patch on their sleeve proclaiming them to be qualified or even "certified" coaches. From the behavior I have seen, I'm not so sure these programs work for the benefit of youngsters.

I don't think that there is a program or a formula for the ideal coach, in part because kids vary so much in personality, motivation, and skills – a variance that becomes more pronounced as kids get older. But the following list – while perhaps not definitive – provides a few guidelines for evaluating a coach.

- **Look for a coach who likes kids.** Often you can get a sense of this by observing the coach with his own children. Kids are very perceptive. They get a feel for a coach right away, and react accordingly. The worst thing you can do is force your child to stay in a program with a coach who does not really care for the kids, but cares a great deal about his own goal of winning a championship. This type of behavior does not usually change over time.

- **Look for a coach who is knowledgeable about baseball.** This knowledge may have come from playing baseball, but be aware that the best coaches were not necessarily the best players. Most of the great coaches and managers I have worked with over the years were not outstanding as players. They struggled to learn and achieve; therefore they understand kids who struggle to perform. Still, it is essential that the coach understand the fundamentals of the game. It is also essential that he be able to analyze and break down the skills for learning purposes.

⦿ **Look for a coach who is a gifted teacher, who creates an environment in which learning is enjoyable.** Instead of official "certification patches," he needs the intuitive understanding that he will have gained from teaching his own children at home. His teaching will be practical, not theoretical, and infused with common sense and personal warmth. Ask yourself: does he look happy to be at practice? If the coach is enjoying the experience, the kids probably are, too.

⦿ **Look for a coach who gives the kids a positive experience every day.** It might be a pizza to reward a hard practice or a simple comment like "That's the best we've hit all year." Parents can evaluate this not only by observing their kids at practice, but also by talking about it afterward. Even with the best coaches, there will be some bad days. But not many.

⦿ **Look for a coach who involves parents.** As a parent, you should want to participate, so you need a coach who encourages your participation

– not just on the sidelines during games, but on the field during practice. Avoid the kind of reception I got when I went to have lunch with my son when he was in second grade. The teacher met me at the door and told me they didn't need me there. My son did not return to that school the next year. If the coach does not welcome your participation, he is either insecure about his ability or way too rigid in his program.

⦿ **Look for a coach with a lot of patience.** This probably goes without saying, but the coach must be patient and tolerant – no matter the age of the kids. He has to be patient with the younger players because of their inability and short attention span, and patient with the older kids because they are trying to establish their independence and everything must be justified to them. The coach must also be patient with the parents and their concerns.

⦿ **Look for a coach who listens.** Most of us are talkers, not listeners. In a hectic, fast-moving environment like sports, listening is not always the mode of operation. But a coach must be able to listen, to hear, and to respond. Young players make a lot of comments and ask a lot of questions, sometimes about things that have nothing to do with baseball. A coach who listens in those situations is a coach who will also get the most effort and desire out of his players.

⦿ **Look for a coach who has a sense of humor.** If the coach doesn't see the humor in youngsters' mistakes, he will need counseling before the year is over. Humor can't be confused with sarcasm. Kids must know that the coach respects effort. You don't laugh at them, but you do laugh with them.

⦿ **Look for a coach who treats kids as individuals.** Kids are very different from each other – physically, mentally, and emotionally. In leading 12 to 15 kids toward the same goal, the coach must know that individuals have their own keys, and he must know which keys motivate each player.

BOBBY COX
Manager, Atlanta Braves

- ★ 2nd in wins among active managers, 15th in history
- ★ American League Manager of the Year, 1982
- ★ National League Manager of the Year, 1991, 1993, 1999
- ★ World Series winner, 1995
- ★ Record nine consecutive Division titles
- ★ Five World Series appearances
- ★ Father of eight

I came from a baseball family in Selma, California. I started playing baseball at eight years old and played pretty much year-round. I played in the first Little League in Selma, which was organized by my father and his seven brothers.

Even so, my dad encouraged me to play all sports, and I played a lot of basketball and football. In fact, I received several football scholarship offers and didn't finally specialize in baseball until I was signed by the Los Angeles Dodgers in 1959. Coming up, I played second base, shortstop, and also pitched. I was in the majors before I became a third baseman, which is what I played for the Yankees.

Obviously, I grew up in a great baseball environment, thanks to my dad and uncles. Their attitudes were always positive; they knew how to look for the good things, and they always stressed the fun of the game. My dad, especially, never got down on me, which I think is very important.

Of all the things I learned from baseball, maybe the most important was the team concept. You know, some kids are going to think they are better than others, but they have to learn to put their egos aside and put the team first. And part of supporting the team is learning to encourage your teammates and never to degrade them.

I also learned to play to win. Winning gets more important as you get up into high school, and you don't want to be satisfied with losing. Of course, you are going to lose some games, and the key here is that losing is acceptable IF you have given it everything you've got. In a nutshell, I'd say: "Play to win, but if you lose, deal with it." Never let a negative attitude set in.

I think the most important thing for parents to remember is to be supportive, never negative. The kids know when they've made mistakes. You don't need to point them out. Parents should also appreciate and respect the time and effort the coaches are putting into the game.

As for getting their kids into the right program, I realize this can be a problem. It's unfortunate that parents don't get to interview the coaches. In fact, these days the coaches often interview the parents, and the parents just feel fortunate to get their kids in the program at all. But what parents can do, and should do, is monitor the attitude of the coach, monitor his behavior, and make sure their kids are in a good environment.

Also, I think it's important for parents never to force their kids into baseball. Even my dad, as a coach, never put any pressure on me, but he helped me have a great time in baseball. I try to be the same way with my kids. If they want to play, that's wonderful. And I hope they have as much fun as I did.

As for coaches, I think they need to remember several things in particular:

⦿ They have to make the game fun for the kids. Even the hard work of practice should be fun, and the kids should not be worked to death. Part of making it fun is giving the kids lots of encouragement. Effort should rewarded, not just results.

⦿ Second, coaches should demonstrate a solid knowledge of baseball and be good teachers of the fundamentals. But, even more important, they should never "show up" the kids, especially in front of their peers. Even on the professional level, my coaches would never do that.

⦿ Third, coaches must have self-control . . . absolutely no yelling and screaming at the kids. Coaches are showing kids how to behave, not just how to play ball.

◉ Fourth, coaches have to remember to give every
   kid some attention.

It's also absolutely necessary that coaches have
great communication with parents. I think in many
cases that would prevent the problem we sometimes have with disruptive parents at the ballpark.

   Along the same lines, I think we should do away
with "All-Stars" and other such awards among the
younger teams. This kind of recognition often con-
tributes to the problems between parents and coaches that make the negative headlines. Also, these
awards can make kids who don't get them think
they're not very good, when, actually, they're too
young to know if they're any good or not. Believe
me, high school is way soon enough to start thinking
about individual awards.

⊙ **Look for a coach who is dedicated to helping kids become better.** First, the coach must be able to recognize where kids are in order to help them get to the next level. As we have said from the beginning, kids must have fun in baseball. It is much easier to have fun if you are getting better as you play. You can evaluate this quality in the coach by listening to his comments to his players, by noting how he compliments performance and encourages improvement.

⊙ **Look for a coach who knows the real meaning of winning.** A good coach will not let his players focus exclusively on the scoreboard. Especially with the younger players, winning should be evaluated in terms of effort – and enjoyment.

This list should help you find the right coach or, in the event that you have no choice, help you evaluate the coach for whom your child is playing. In many cases, the coach may prove to be less than ideal, and then the critical question becomes: Do I, as a parent, have assets to contribute to the play-

ers, assets that might complement the coach's talents and help to offset his liabilities?

But the bottom line is simple. When their kids
quit baseball, most parents blame the coaching.

III. LEARN ABOUT BASEBALL

I heard a very disappointing comment recently
from a parent of a young baseball player. "I would
help the coach, but I need to cut the grass," he said.
My comment to him: "It's a matter of priorities." I
wanted to say several other things. Is anything
more important than the welfare of your children?
Is anything more important than spending time
with your children? Would the grass grow to an
uncuttable height if you waited two hours? But the
truth is, parents have all kinds of reasons not to
spend time learning what they need to know about
the game. Priorities will be discussed later.

There are two fundamental things parents need
to learn about baseball. First, baseball is a very difficult game to play. It involves so many motor
skills: hand-eye coordination, balance, reaction
time, agility, strength, speed, and quickness. In the
early '70s, research conducted to determine which
sport required the most athletic skills indicated
quite conclusively that baseball players were the
best all-around athletes. In fact, the toughest single
skill in sports is hitting a pitched baseball with a

bat. So be tolerant when your youngster swings and misses the ball. And while you're at it, make sure your beginning player has a hitting T available for practice.

Second, parents themselves should learn the basic skills – throwing, catching, and hitting – so that they can practice these skills with their child. For example, you can work on catching with two hands, a technique that increases the likelihood of a good catch and also puts the player in better position to throw the ball.

Or take hitting. In working on this skill, parents can help their child focus on one simple concept: See the ball and hit the ball. One thing at a time. When you ask one of the top professional hitters in the world what he thinks about when he steps into the batter's box, he will say, "See the ball, hit the ball."

It's a good idea for you parents to practice throwing and catching against the wall, and to go to a local batting cage and practice hitting the ball, before you do these things with your child. By learning these basic skills, you will 1) learn how difficult the skills are; 2) learn how to teach your child; and 3) discover some ways to make the learning process more fun. You will also become a better, more supportive spectator during practice and games.

IV. GET YOUR PRIORITIES IN ORDER

Do you hope to live vicariously through your child's experiences? Or do you hope to make youth baseball a positive, meaningful experience for your youngster? Perhaps you need to evaluate your own purpose for getting involved in youth baseball and how it fits within your other priorities for the growth and development of your child. There are any number of reasons for getting kids into youth baseball. Some are valid and wholesome. Some indicate misplaced priorities.

A couple of tidbits of information here that might cause you to review your own priorities. As I noted earlier, 75 percent of players drop out by 13 years old. Many of these kids were forced to play by parents, and many of them played 70 to 80 games on traveling teams and burned out on baseball. Also, if you're counting on a pro career for your child, remember that of all those who continue to play, get better, and sign with professional teams, less than 2 percent make it to the major leagues.

Obviously, your priority as a parent should be to

provide your child with a variety of experiences as he is growing up. If youth baseball happens to be one of those experiences, your priority should be to make it a fun and worthwhile experience. Keeping your kid occupied so you can have more time to yourself should not be on the list of priorities.

TOM GLAVINE

Pitcher, Atlanta Braves

★ National League Cy Young Award Winner, 1991 and 1998
★ Major Leagues' winningest left-handed pitcher in the 1990s
★ Seven-time All-Star
★ Five-time 20-game winner
★ Four-time Silver Slugger
★ Father of four

I guess you could say I started playing baseball at an early age – seven years old. But I started playing hockey when I was five. In fact, I was drafted by the Los Angeles Kings in the NHL and planned to go to college first. But then I was drafted by the Atlanta Braves and decided to be a baseball player. That seemed like the better opportunity. But it was not until being drafted that I really "specialized" in baseball.

Playing baseball as a kid, I was lucky to have tremendous support from my parents and my coaches. Both Mom and Dad really encouraged me, and we did a lot of pitching and catching in the backyard. My parents laid down two rules, both of which, I think, had a lot to do with my success:

First: do well in school, because only then would I be allowed to participate in sports; and

Second: be smiling when you go out to play the game, and be smiling when the game is over, win or lose.

Luckily, my coaches reinforced this message. I *never* played on a team where the primary emphasis was on winning. My coaches believed that we were there to (1) have fun and (2) learn how to play the game. Winning was great, but we always put more emphasis on getting better and developing our skills. A very important by-product of this attitude is that I was never afraid to make mistakes. We always understood that that's how you get better.

With the help of parents and coaches, I got a lot from my youth baseball experience. Probably the most important things I learned were the "life skills" that had to do with belonging to a team: the value of teammates, cooperation, communication, commitment to a team goal, and depending on others to reach that goal. The fact that I lived in a neighborhood with a lot of older kids helped me come to understand some of these things.

My advice to parents would be: "Do what my parents did!" Seriously, I think the only really important things parents have to remember are to be supportive and to remind their kids that the game is supposed to be fun.

The one thing I would warn parents against is burdening their kids with their own dreams and ambitions. I see too many parents who seem to be trying to fulfill their own lives by nurturing a potential "big leaguer." And please, don't force your kids into the game. If my kids want to play, fine. If they don't, fine.

My dad taught me quite a few lessons that other dads could probably pass along as well: he taught me the value of hard work; he taught me to compete; he taught me to appreciate how tough it is to play baseball well. But most important, he taught me to remember these words: "There is always somebody better than you."

I would also say to parents, if you have any choice in the program you get your kid in, try to find one that, first, offers a fun environment, and, second, that emphasizes good instruction and skills development. Because after all, the game is more fun if you know how to play.

To coaches I would say one thing in particular: Get rid of the "win at all costs" attitude. It's harmful, and it makes no sense. For kids, the game is about having fun and learning the basics.

Youth baseball is for the kids' development, not the coaches' self-development. It's not the place for the coaches' self-promotion either.

For me, winning became really important in high school. I mean, I always hated losing, and I always played to win, but my emphasis was on enjoying the game and getting better. Honestly, I never thought about professional athletics until the end of my high school career.

The thing is, if the coaches can get over the idea that winning is all-important, and if parents can keep in mind that youth baseball is supposed to be fun, then we will have solved the problem of disruptive behavior at the ballpark. Again, you've got to have the right priorities. If the coach has instilled that "win at all costs" attitude, he's asking for problems.

V. SUPPORT YOUR YOUNGSTER

Your primary role in the youth baseball program is to support your youngster; following that, your role is to support the coaches and the program.

Even though your physical presence at practice and games may change as your child gets older, your emotional support should not change, and may even get stronger as the years pass.

With the younger players – five to eight years old – your support *and* physical presence is absolutely essential. But note: I said *support*, not pressure. I will never forget when I coached T-ball and one of my better players – one who actually could catch, throw, and hit on occasion – came to me one day with tears in his eyes. "I sure hope my dad doesn't come to the game today," he said. I felt so bad. I knew that wasn't what he meant. He wanted his dad to be supportive, but not so critical. His dad would throw his cap against the fence and yell at the top of his lungs. Eventually, he would go and sit in the car until the game was over. After much thought, I asked this dad to be my assistant coach – even though the other folks who helped me were skeptical. It worked out fine. Once the father realized how tough the game is to play, he quit all the yelling. Most important, the kid started enjoying the games.

My goal was to have such strong support for the youngsters that they couldn't wait for the next season to start. We wanted at least one family member at every practice and at games. To me, the idea of car pooling, so that parents only showed up when it was their turn to drive, was reprehensible. The parents of my players knew pretty clearly how I felt about their tennis game or golf game taking precedence over their child's practice. How can you help your child practice at home if you never attend the team's practice?

As young players get older and begin to try to be more independent, they seem not to want our parental support anymore. In reality, as they are physically pushing you away, they are still seeking your emotional support. Your child's need to have you there for him, in spirit if not in body, never goes away.

Remember, too, that in competitive sports like baseball, tough losses are part of the experience.

When things are going great, kids become pretty independent. But during times of adversity in baseball, kids need their parents. They need perspective, they need encouragement, sometimes they just need a shoulder to cry on. The need to share a victory and the joy of basking in parental pride is balanced by the need for gentle comfort, reassurance, and reinforcement on those days of defeat. Parents and their youngsters are lucky that youth baseball offers both of these experiences.

VI. KNOW WHEN YOUR CHILD IS READY

Rule to remember: "It's the timeliness, not the earliness."

Knowing "when" has to be the toughest decision for a parent to make. Sometimes *our* need for our child to play baseball outweighs our child's need to play, and, as a result, our youngsters are starting earlier and earlier. Forty-four years ago I played in the first youth baseball program in West Knoxville, Tennessee. I was 12. My starting so young was a source of local controversy. Now we are starting kids in baseball at four years old.

We're not only starting early; we're specializing early. Some parents are training their sons to become pitchers beginning at age eight. We have nutritionists and weight trainers for preteens. Kids in seventh and eighth grade are taking dietary supplements to increase size and strength. Scary, but true. Here are a couple of personal experiences.

One November, a mother called to ask me to fly to Ft. Lauderdale to work with her son. He had lost the "killer instinct." He was still a winner, but not a superstar. Could I please sit and talk with him?

When we got down to the vital statistics, she told me her son would turn seven in January. After I expressed my opinion to this parent, the conversation ended abruptly.

Another mother called to ask me to work with her 11-year-old daughter. The mom lived in Chicago, but I wouldn't need to travel because her daughter lived in Atlanta. During the conversation I learned that this 11-year-old had lived away from home for five years – in a different city each year with a different coach. Her parents saw her at Christmas, but not every Christmas. I accused this mom of child abuse and told her if I lived in Chicago, I would try to have her arrested. Strong language to use with an ignorant parent, I suppose. But a parent who says a child is willing to give up everything for a sport at the age of four is a parent who has been severely warped by the "earlier is better" theory.

We had one parent who changed his son's birth certificate when he was only three so that he could play in a soccer league for five-year-olds. The father's explanation was his son would "learn to be tough" by being with older children.

As parents, we need to understand about "critical learning periods." Research on how and when youngsters learn motor skills has produced interesting results. Tests on twins, for example, has shown that if you teach one twin a set of motor skills at six years old and teach the other twin at nine, their skills will be equal when tested at age 12.

I personally know professional baseball players on Major League teams who started baseball as late as seniors in college. Most great players played several sports through high school before settling on baseball.

The theory of critical learning periods simply states that there is a time in a child's life when he is ready physically, socially, and emotionally to compete in sport. Most kids are categorized in youth baseball according to age, and consequently are placed on teams according to physical development. No consideration is given to social and emotional factors, and many kids who are physically ready to play are not ready at all for actual competition, or for winning and losing, or for the social dynamics required to participate on a team.

Too often parents don't understand this concept

until their son has become discouraged and quit baseball. You don't have to push your son into baseball. Wait until he shows an interest in playing the game. The logical sequence in the level of competition will keep the young player interested. Don't be discouraged if your child doesn't play baseball at eight years old. Sending kids off to hitting instructors or to special pitching and catching camps will not make a difference if they are not ready to play.

VII. EXPECT POSITIVE THINGS TO HAPPEN

You have to realize how important your own attitude is – that your attitude actually influences events. Realize that what you expect from the baseball environment is what you will get. That's why you should expect to have fun. Always look for the good things when you watch youngsters play baseball. Look for them, enjoy them, and reinforce them. In fact, if you're not expecting good things to happen, then don't go to the baseball field at all.

We must understand the potential impact negative expectations can have on a young baseball player. This topic will also be discussed in the sections for coaches and athletes. Admittedly, it takes a conscious effort to have positive expectations in an environment where so many mistakes are made every day. Nevertheless, it is absolutely critical that positive expectations permeate the baseball environment

The fact is that parents begin to project negative expectations almost from the time of their child's birth. If we could calculate the number of times we say "no" to our youngsters and add the number of negative comments made by teachers, coaches, and others in our youngster's environment, the total would approach 189,000 times during the first 18 years. Because of this conditioning, it becomes human nature for our emotions to drift toward negativity. Kids will begin to spend all their time and energy trying to not fail, trying to not get embarrassed, trying to not disappoint their parents.

This is the very reason we must project positive expectations to our young players. If they strike out, maybe they took some good cuts. If the ball goes between their legs, maybe they got in the right position to make the play. If the young ones hit the ball and run in the wrong direction, it's a positive that they ran. You see, there is always something positive that you can discuss on the way home – always something they did to deserve a hot dog and a soft drink.

Expectations are very fragile. Positive expectations that we project on Monday mean nothing on Tuesday. We start over every day. It takes a lot of positive reinforcement to build up a kid's psyche, but only one failed play to tear it down.

There are no guarantees. But by expecting positive things to happen, we definitely increase the probability of good things happening.

VIII. HAVE FUN WITH YOUR YOUNGSTER

We have talked a lot in this section about how important it is to provide a fun experience for young players, about fun as the primary incentive for younger players to continue playing.

Perhaps the one thing we have neglected to emphasize is how important it is for parents to have fun during the youth baseball experience. Youth baseball is for kids to play, but for everyone to enjoy.

Obviously, the easiest way to have fun is to be totally dedicated to the environment, focused on watching and supporting your youngster. Just how do you clear your mind of all its daily concerns so that you can relax and enjoy a baseball practice or game? As a mom, how do you redirect your energy from working or taking care of your other children to giving 100 percent to your young baseball player for the next two hours? As a dad, how do you separate yourself from workday frustrations and pressures to give your total attention to your youngster?

The answer to these questions lies in the concept

of balance. Balance in your life does not mean equal hours at work and at home. Balance deals with the quality of time. Balance means learning how to be at work when you're at work, and how to be *not at work* when you're not at work. Oddly, this is most difficult for those of us, whether moms or dads, who work from home. At the home office, work becomes too convenient, and it requires tremendous self-discipline to mentally get away from it and focus on your personal life. But achieving balance is unquestionably the key to having fun, both at work and not at work.

Here are a couple of tips for getting where you need to be for the youth baseball experience – and if you find you're creating some balance in your life at the same time, so much the better:

◉ Set daily goals that can be accomplished within a time frame, without rolling over into baseball time.

◉ Slow down 30 minutes to one hour before baseball starts. Take a deep breath and give yourself a mental break.

- Talk with your child about what he expects at practice or at the game.

- If you are having a difficult time focusing, mentally go back to a previous practice or game that was fun to watch.

- Make it your firm intention to relax and enjoy. Let the coach do the coaching and the kids do the playing.

- Plan to learn something about your child in the next two hours. Key on taking something positive from the field, something you can laugh at and talk about with your child on the way home.

- Reward yourself and your young players with a quick stop for dessert on the way home.

- Guard against scheduling other obligations too tightly around the baseball experience. Give yourself time to get ready, and give yourself time to emotionally and physically "back down" after baseball. As a parent, you may have pre-performance anxiety just as your child does. This anxiety usually goes down to a manageable level during performance, so that you can enjoy the event. But after the game or practice, your post-performance anxiety may actually become higher than the pre-performance level. So make sure to give yourself a "cooling-off" period.

I'm sure there are other things you can do to prepare to have fun, but this list should give you a start.

IX. KEEP WINNING IN PERSPECTIVE

Winning is a fascinating concept, and everybody talks about it. But if winning means scoring more runs in a game than your opponent, what about T-ball games where, in many leagues, the score is not kept? The kids play for an hour and go home. The object here is for every kid to feel that he has won, and when that happens, winning takes on its proper meaning.

As a parent, you must move beyond the score-board concept of winning and losing. Admittedly, winning changes in definition as kids get older. But in the meantime, you should be talking to your son about "winning effort"; you should be dealing with the process and not so much the end result. Younger players don't really understand winning and losing anyway. Several years ago we were making a video tape for parents and coaches, and we were shooting footage in a huge youth baseball park in California. After the game we would interview players, who were between five and seven years old. The answers to our questions were very revealing. Over 85 percent of the youngsters didn't know if they won or lost, and didn't seem to care. Over 95 percent stated that they had a good time. Yet these kids learned all the basic skills and felt like winners. Winning was participation.

Every day you take your young athlete to the baseball field, you should expect a win-win situation. You win by watching and supporting his efforts, and he wins by playing the game. When players get older and get involved in higher-level performance and winning strategy, you, as a parent, must think about the game from two perspectives. First, did the team win or lose the game on the scoreboard? Second, did your son display a winning effort, even during adversity? Winning certainly builds on winning, but losing can create some valuable teaching moments for you as a parent.

Losing enables you to talk about "best effort" and about recovery from adversity. It shows kids the importance of developing the kind of winning attitude that helps them recover from losing. Your own attitude around your child is a prerequisite to this effort.

X. KNOW YOUR YOUNGSTER'S GOALS

Isn't it interesting how our adult goals take precedence over our kids' goals in youth baseball? Under the guise of doing "what is best for the child," some parents pay huge fees for private instruction in the hope that their son will either get drafted out of high school by a professional team or, at least, get a college scholarship. I really think most parents do a super job of supporting their kids' goals; it's just that small percentage who get off track and then make things difficult for other parents who feel they have to "keep up."

Parents call every week wanting to have me work with their young athletes. Often they are trying to get the "edge" before college coaches start recruiting their child – even though these kids might be as young as 12 years old. When I ask the kids why they want the "mental coaching," some look shocked, others look puzzled, and still others honestly say, "My parents think I need it." The fact is that in most cases the kids' own goals are simply to play the game and have a good time being with their friends.

Here's a recent example. A parent called to
request a session for his young son, whom the parent described as "potentially a great hitter, just in
need for a confidence boost." When I talked with this
young player, I found that *his* goal was to get "one
hit" during the season. The kid was serious.
Unfortunately, so was the parent, who had somehow
inflated his child's goal to fit with his own vision.

Some kids play initially to get the designated
"treat" after the game; some for the reward of fast
food on the way home. We adults may have trouble
understanding such simple – even trivial – goals.
But we don't have to understand them. We just
have to support them.

I've had kids in the field spend a lot of time trying to tie their shoe. Baseballs flying all around
them. But they had a goal and were focused on
accomplishing that task. I respected the focus, the
concentration, and the persistence. After they suc-
ceeded, we talked about pursuing other goals –
such as catching, throwing, and hitting – with that
same intensity. The response was very positive.
Parents on the sideline are tempted to yell at their
child to forget the shoe and pay attention to the

game, and, as a result, the child might end up accomplishing nothing. If the child's immediate goal is to get his shoe tied properly, let's respect that. Then we can move on to the next goal.

A kid's long-range goal is likely to be getting through a *game*, not a season and certainly not a 10-year career. Some just want to get dirty, as a visible sign that they played. Parents need to be "goal-setting consultants" for kids in baseball. Let's just spend more time asking kids what they want to get out of baseball.

REGGIE SANDERS
Outfielder, Arizona Diamondbacks

★ All-Star, 1995
★ 3rd in MVP balloting, 1995
★ Hit three home runs in one game
★ Father of two

I started playing baseball pretty early, at about six years old. All my uncles played every weekend, so baseball was in my family before I was born.

I ran track and played football, too, but I began to really focus on baseball in my early high school years. As for my position, I thought I was focusing on shortstop. I was always a shortstop. I was drafted as a shortstop by the Reds. But it turned out they already had a good young shortstop, Barry Larkin, so they put me on a fast track to the outfield, and I've been an outfielder ever since.

I was fortunate to always have good coaches as a kid. I learned the important things: the fundamentals of the game, how to play with other kids, how to be a part of a team. But our coaches always emphasized the fun of the game. They were challenging and motivating, but they made the game fun. Even the competitive drills we did were fun.

Of course, I always played to win, and as I got older, especially in college, winning got to be pretty important. But as a kid I just really liked to play and didn't worry too much about winning or losing. In fact, I probably didn't really learn to deal with losing until I got to the majors. With so many games in a season, you really have to accept that you're going to lose some games and keep yourself on an even keel.

My advice to parents is: "Support, but don't push." More important than anything, I would say, is to let your kids be themselves.

If your child does want to get into baseball, you ought to do a little homework on the coach's background. Talk to other parents whose kids have been with this coach or this program and see what their experience has been. Be careful not to buy into a slick sales pitch, which some coaches are good at.

I also have a suggestion for parents on game day. If you have something to tell your kid, some advice or instruction, be sure to say it *before the game*. Once the game starts, you have to let 'em play.

To coaches, I would offer several tips:

- Get to know each kid's personality and treat every one as an individual.

- Teach the fundamentals – throwing, catching, hitting – and don't go overboard.

- Be a good listener.

- Be a helper.

- Have fun and enjoy the experience.

- And finally, don't watch too much professional baseball.

The problem youth baseball has with parents who get out of hand is really unfortunate. It's terrible to see kids suffer because of their parents' behavior. The kids really can't do anything about it themselves, and you can see them get really frustrated and embarrassed by their rowdy parents.

It's up to the coach to meet with all his players *and* all the parents on the very first day. He's got to lay down his rules, make sure everybody understands them, and stick to them. Being consistent is the key.

But at the same time, the coach shouldn't make it a defensive encounter. Most parents want to contribute, and the coach should encourage that and let them know what he needs from them. The parents are there, you can't ignore them. The best thing is to make an effort to include them.

XI. BE OBJECTIVE ABOUT YOUR CHILD'S ROLE ON THE TEAM

This is particularly tough for the parent who is also the coach. One of the most frequently asked questions from parents is, "Should I coach my own kid?" My answer is, "As long as you don't coach him on the way to the park, on the way home, and at the family dinner table!" Easier said than done. See the "Coaches" section for more discussion of this topic.

The first thing for parents to understand is what a great environment youth baseball offers. It's a place for kids to learn to interact with their peers, to learn self-discipline and persistence, to learn how to recover from adversity and how to be a team member. The bottom line is that this environment can do a tremendous job of helping kids to develop a strong, positive self-concept.

The second thing to remember is it takes a very long time to build a self-concept and only a few seconds to destroy it. A negative comment, especially from a parent, can be devastating to a young athlete. Understand that in trying to develop his self-concept, your child may just want to be on the team, to wear a uniform. (As one parent told me in T-ball, his son couldn't wait until they gave out the team costumes.) This child sees his role as simply *being on the team*. We need to respect that. I've seen parents who are embarrassed to say their son is on the bench. But think about this for a second. Do you want your child on the field when he doesn't want to be there? He may feel that he needs more practice before he plays. The last thing you need is for him to get embarrassed or, worse, to get injured.

As kids get older and continue to play, their confidence increases and they want to play to show you their skills. At that point, you need to get them into a situation in which they are going to play. But in the meantime, be patient with your kid. *Ask him how he sees his role on the team.* If that role is not being fulfilled, then have a conversation with the coach. You may indeed find that your young player is not in the most suitable program. It's a good idea for everyone to have an understanding of the participation policies up front. But if your youngster is content, don't be the negative spark that lights the flame of discontent.

Always be positive, and respect kids for what talent they bring to the game. Help them to understand that everybody on the team has a role, and what it means to be a team member.

XII. NEVER LOSE TRACK OF WHOM YOUTH BASEBALL WAS ORGANIZED FOR

Just a quick reminder. If you can work on these first 11 ideas over the course of a baseball season, chances are very good that your child will benefit significantly from his experience. However, this suggestion, No. 12, cannot stretch over time. You, as parents, must commit before the baseball experience ever starts to the idea that youth baseball was organized for the kids. After all, if it had been organized for parents, we would play and our children would watch.

PARENTS' QUESTIONS & ANSWERS

Here are some of the questions parents ask most fre-
quently in my youth baseball seminars. I hope you'll
find your questions answered here.

1. What do you think about specializing in positions at an early age in baseball?

I feel strongly that youngsters should have a broad experience in youth sports. The more sports they play, the better prepared they will be to select and specialize when they get to high school. The same principle holds true for specializing in different positions within baseball. Kids should be permitted to play every position. They may not become highly skilled at every position, but they will develop an appreciation for other players' talents. As they grow physically, their size may dictate the position they play. Also, whether they are left- or right-handed will eliminate certain positions as they play at higher levels. For example, in the lower levels, throwing preference is not an issue, but as they progress, catching, third base, shortstop, and second base are eliminated for left-handers. The one exception here is that I would not encourage every player to try pitching. It is both incredible and scary how many young players – often as young as 14 years old – need elbow operations because of too much pitching, usually due to incorrect mechanics.

2. At what age should kids start playing competitive baseball?

If the focus is healthy (i.e., participation, fun, basic skills, etc.), then T-ball is a super experience for kids, even at six years old. As kids get to be older, though, the focus changes. I have a real problem with parents who try to get their kids into competition too early for the wrong reasons, and with parents who try to enroll their kids in programs for older kids. We call this "playing up," and it's not a good idea.

CHIPPER JONES
Third Baseman, Atlanta Braves

★ National League MVP, 1999
★ Silver Slugger Award, 1999, 2000
★ Four-time All-Star
★ World Series Champion, 1995
★ Father of two

My father was a terrific baseball player, and I'm sure he got me started as soon as I could hold a ball or bat, but I guess I started playing organized baseball when I was about eight years old.

Growing up, though, I played whatever sport was in season – basketball, football, soccer. In fact, I was an All-State wide receiver in high school. But baseball was always my passion; I played other sports just to stay busy.

In terms of my position in baseball, I specialized early. My dad was a shortstop, so I was a shortstop. Always a shortstop. Of course, I'm no longer a short-stop, so maybe specializing early isn't so important.

Baseball was always great fun for me. In fact, it

still is. And that's how it should be, especially for kids. Kids today seem like they're in too much of a hurry to grow up. They need to have fun while they can.

Of course winning gets to be important, but it shouldn't be for the young kids learning the game. For me, winning started to take on importance in high school, which makes sense. But again, it seems to be happening younger and younger. There is too much emphasis on championships – and also too much emphasis on things like All Stars – at the younger ages. These things can actually turn kids away from the game.

My advice to parents stems from the great example my dad set and the great relationship I had with him. He was always completely supportive but without crossing over that line. For example, he did a lot of coaching, but he would always drop off of any team that I was going to be a member of to avoid any chance of favoritism.

So my advice to parents is simple: be the parents,

be the role model, be there for your kids. Everything starts with you. Don't rely on other people's influence. And absolutely do not depend on some professional coach or athlete to raise your child.

What I would tell coaches is sort of the other side of the coin. Sometimes parents want to give up too much responsibility, and sometimes, I think, coaches want to take on too much responsibility. I see too many coaches that take their positions way too seriously.

More than anything, I would remind coaches that it's only a game, that it's supposed to be fun. Honestly, sometimes they might have just one real baseball player on their whole team, so why take it so seriously? The coaches, I think, need to relax . . . and have a lot of patience.

3. What do you think about baseball camps for youngsters?

There are some excellent camps available, but you should do some thorough investigation before committing your kids to the experience. Check the instructors, the safety regulations, the activities, and the ages of participants. Most colleges have well-supervised camps, and you might also contact the United States Baseball Federation for more information. Just be realistic about your expectations from these camps – and about your child's expectations.

4. What's my role as a parent in youth baseball?

Support and consolation during adversity, and encouragement during the good times. Help your youngster to have fun. Select the right program and support that program. It may be that your primary role is transportation, *and* staying to watch during practice and games.

5. What can I do to get my child interested in baseball?

Simply provide exposure, perhaps by playing baseball with him at home or by taking him to games. Many times youngsters are reluctant to venture into "strange" new areas, but when they try a new game, they find that it can be fun. Don't be afraid to throw the ball in the backyard with your child. Get a bat and let him hit the ball. Kids love to hit things.

6. My child likes to play, but doesn't seem to be bothered by losing. What can I do?

Perhaps your child is content to be a part of the team and is not yet a strong competitor. It's also possible that he may not want to become a great competitor in baseball or other sports. It's wise to let him develop his own competitive instinct – without pushing.

7. My kid cries when he loses. What can I do?

Lend him your shoulder. Crying is one of the

healthier emotional outlets for us. Children are to be admired because they have very few inhibitions. Disappointment at losing is a natural feeling. When the crying has subsided, then it's time to talk with your child about lessons learned, to turn the loss into a positive experience. The late Jim Valvano, basketball coach at North Carolina State, made a great comment in his last speech before dying from cancer: "Everyday we have to laugh, we have to cry, and we have to think!" Don't inhibit children who stretch their emotions.

8. How can I make sure that my child is in a safe environment?

Make sure his team uses approved equipment. Make sure the coaches have had some emergency care training. Don't hesitate to ask questions on these issues, and take the time to observe practice. Most leagues have standard safety rules, and you should be sure you're comfortable with the implementation of these standards prior to letting your child participate.

9. My eight-year-old wants to be a switch-hitter. He's a much better hitter right-handed. What should I do?

If he wants to try switch-hitting, the earlier the better. Since he's just now learning to hit, why not let him try from both sides? He will be better from one side than the other, but this should not be a reason for prohibiting him from working on the weaker side. If he works on it now, he can learn correctly early as opposed to developing bad habits and trying to correct them later. We have players in professional baseball who learn to switch-hit in their 20s, or who finally give it up.

10. How can I judge my kid's talent for the future?

You can't. Some kids develop quickly and never get any better. Some kids take longer to develop. You need to avoid the "traveling team" and "scholarship" talk with your young players. Just encourage them to play one day at a time, to keep learning, and to play hard every day. I've known professional baseball pitchers who never pitched until they were in the major leagues. I knew one major league pitcher who never played baseball until his senior year in college.

11. When should my son start throwing curve balls and split-finger pitches?

This is a controversial question. Based on recent research into throwing arm problems in young pitchers, indications are that kids should not throw breaking pitches until the mid to late teens. Actually, the two things your son should be thinking about are (1) building up arm strength by throwing straight, and (2) learning how to throw strikes. It does a young pitcher no good to throw four different pitches without throwing any of the four consistently for strikes.

I work with pitchers in the major leagues, pitchers at the highest level, who work every day on developing new pitches. Your son has plenty of time to learn the different pitches.

LARRY ROTHSCHILD

Manager, Tampa Bay Devil Rays

★ 4th year as Devil Rays' manager
★ 25-year career in professional baseball
★ 11-year playing career
★ Father of three

I've been playing baseball since before I can remember, but I played all sports growing up – especially football and hockey. I didn't really focus on baseball until I was in college, which was when I also started to focus on pitching. But I also played shortstop and second base.

The person who influenced me the most, I guess, was my older brother. He was a really good player, and I would watch him and try to play like him. My parents were both very supportive also, but without trying to push me into the game.

We had a great time. This was back when we would just show up at the park, choose sides, and play. Make our own rules. Totally informal. Just playing the game. It seems like you can't do that anymore. Either there's not a safe place to play, or there's too much supervision and organization.

And of course, who won or lost wasn't important. That would come later, in high school, I guess. I don't remember being concerned about it before that time. What I remember is having fun playing the game.

My advice to parents is simply to make sure their kids are having fun in baseball. That's what it's about. In fact, with my own children, I encourage them to play baseball and other sports. But if it gets to be so serious that the fun goes away, then I'll pull them out.

I also think parents need to make sure that the coach and the whole league share this same attitude – that it's supposed to be fun and not taken too seriously.

Of course, sometimes it's the parents whose attitudes need fixing. Parents, too, need to understand what the game is about, and they need to accept that the coach is in charge. There is no excuse for some incidents you hear about. An occasional "weekend without parents" might be a good idea if problems persist.

But, you know, it seems a shame that such issues even come up. Everything seems to have gotten so complicated. Maybe we should go back to the days when you go to the park, pick teams, and play baseball.

Coaches should also think primarily about making the game fun for the kids – for a very practical reason. If the kids are having fun, they will want to learn the basic skills. If you want them to stay around long enough to learn how to play the game, you have to make it fun for them.

I would also remind coaches to keep a healthy attitude about winning and losing. After all, the coaches should be having fun, too, and it's hard to do that if you're too caught up in the outcome of the game.

12. What should I expect from private instructors?

Caution: Steer away from an instructor who, upon first glance at your five- or six-year-old, says to you, "This kid is a natural!" or "With my help this kid will be a great player!" or "By the time he is in high school, I can guarantee this kid a scholarship!" Review the answer to No. 10. Don't start private instruction too early. Private instruction says to your eight-year-old, "Mom and Dad are serious about wanting me to be a great player." You are sending the wrong expectations. Baseball is play, not work.

When and if you do make a commitment to use special instruction, be patient in your selection. Do your homework, just as you do in selecting a coach. Background, experience playing and teaching, facilities, and references are all critical. And, of course, your child's perception of the instructor.

13. My kid is afraid to fail. He avoids the tough plays in the field and does not swing at the ball for fear of missing it. What can we do?

Fear of failure is something we all experience – as kids, as parents, as corporate workers, as spouses. Fear of failure actually is an incentive to get better at a task – unless it crosses a psychological barrier and becomes a detriment to performance that can drive you away from that particular endeavor.

It is positive that your son still wants to play, and your first responsibility is to support him every time he swings. Then analyze his skills with the coach, and call attention to his mechanics, to standing in the batter's box, to concentrating. At home, help him develop his swing off the hitting T; then progress to the "soft toss": from the side (you and your son facing each other), underhand-toss balls into the strike zone so he can begin to hit a moving target. Players do this drill for years to keep their "eye" and their coordination.

In regard to fielding tough plays, again break the skill down. Begin with soft grounders and gradually roll them out of reach so he has to dive for the ball. Do this in a soft, grassy area. Teach him how to get to his feet and throw. Again, work with the coach.

The key to overcoming fear of failure is success. In your case, you may have to manufacture success; you may have to spoon-feed success.

14. My son plays high school baseball. He is a good player, but he suffers from great anxiety before games, even though it seems to go away once play starts. Is there anything my wife and I can do to ease his anxiety?

Pre-performance anxiety is a good thing. Every athlete has it. I've seen professional players who get sick before every game. That's at least 162 times a year. Don't call unnecessary attention to the anxiety unless it begins to adversely affect his performance. Anxiety will naturally drop during performance to a controllable level. After games, you may even see his anxiety go up for a period of time, maybe even higher than the pre-performance level. The system needs to "unwind."

15. What do you think is the best sport for young athletes?

All sports are good for developing bodies and minds as long as they are taught properly and approached properly. When children are very young, under 10, physical activities that stress flexibility and endurance – such as soccer, gymnastics, and dance – may be the most beneficial. The most critical point to remember is that young athletes have an opportunity to play various sports and various positions.

A range of sports experience will give the youngster a better background when he decides to specialize and will help him develop speed, agility, flexibility, coordination, balance, and decision-making skills.

That said, baseball provides experience in a great number of motor skills. In fact, good baseball players are probably the best all-around athletes. So, perhaps with some prejudice, my choice would be youth baseball.

16. When he was younger, my son played whatever sport was in season and the sport that the other kids wanted to play. But since he entered high school, he's being encouraged to concentrate on baseball. It's his best sport, and he enjoys it, but shouldn't I encourage him to play other sports as well?

Most of the professional baseball players with whom I work played at least two sports through high school and didn't make their choice to play only baseball until their senior year. On the other hand, if your son has played several sports up to this point and now chooses to play only baseball, that's fine. He simply needs a full understanding of what he is getting by specializing and what he is missing by not playing the other sports.

Readers of the sports pages know of three great high school athletes who played both baseball and football, signed lucrative contracts to play baseball, played several years in the minor leagues, and are now out of baseball and playing quarterback at major universities.

It's finally a personal decision, but my best advice is: general early, specific late. If he has chosen baseball, make sure he gets good instruction and good equipment.

17. My son tells us how well he's doing in practice, but when we show up for games, he gets nervous and performs poorly. What's going on?

You need to realize that if you come to the games but not to practice, you are placing your child under unusual pressure to perform for you. Many kids perform poorly under these conditions. If possible, you really need to attend practices, to simulate the game environment, and to encourage your kid at every opportunity.

You will enjoy watching him learn as much as watching him play, and he will get used to the idea of your watching him. As a result, he will be able to play with emotion during the game, but emotion under control.

18. Should girls play on boys' teams in youth baseball?

Why not? Girls may be even stronger and more coordinated than boys during the formative youth baseball years. Girls have played on youth baseball World Series teams. Softball has grown tremendously for girls, but that does not mean that girls cannot play baseball if they so choose.

Part 2
Tips for Coaches

Youth baseball can either be a wonderful experience or an unpleasant memory. We adults may remember only a few teachers from our formative years, but we'll remember every coach from our youth baseball years, both the good and the bad. In fact, many youngsters learn more about how not to behave from their coach then they learn about how to behave. I cannot emphasize too strongly the critical role of the youth baseball coach in the physical, social, and psychological development of young people.

Parents, for one reason or another, do not always give children the time they need – a circumstance that lends even more value and importance to the structured playtime provided by youth baseball. In this environment, the youth baseball coach often plays the role of substitute parent, not to mention the roles of teacher, counselor, and friend.

Being responsible for the production of a group of employees in a corporate environment pales in comparison to accepting the responsibility that comes with supervising and teaching a group of young baseball players, whether they are five-year-olds or 15-year-olds. When you have these children at the baseball field, you are truly "the man." You can make them love the sport and play it for years (or at least become lifelong fans) or you can drive them out of baseball and perhaps out of any type of competition.

At the risk of oversimplifying a very complicated endeavor, youth baseball coaches need two basic skills: the technical competence to teach the basic skills of the game, and the emotional competence to deal with young people. But more important than your skills is your attitude; you need to be volunteering to coach for all the right reasons.

What do you want to get out of your coaching

experience? What do you want the kids to get? The 12-point list of goals below is the kind of thing I use to establish a plan and get me focused.

- Create a beneficial experience for kids.

- Provide the kids with a healthy and safe environment.

- Teach correct playing techniques.

- Teach kids how to compete and how to cooperate.

- Teach kids the meaning of winning.

- Teach kids to cope in adverse conditions.

- Teach kids how to set and reach goals.

- Teach kids how to develop self-discipline.

- Teach kids to respect other players' talents.

- Teach kids how to play by the rules.

- Help kids develop a lasting appreciation for baseball.

- Always emphasize that baseball is a game, and games should be fun.

How do you establish the kind of environment in which your kids will enable you to accomplish these 12 goals? Simply by winning the kids' confidence from the first day. To help you do that, and to ultimately provide the best baseball experience you can for yourself and your players, I offer the following guidelines for continual self-evaluation.

I. BE A BASEBALL PERSON

Nothing establishes credibility faster than being able to show youngsters how to execute skills, at least at a basic level of competency. When I talk with professional baseball players about the things they remember about their youth baseball coach, invariably I get this kind of response: "He could play the game," or "He didn't just talk about hitting, he could hit." You don't have to throw the ball hard, or hit it long, or make incredible plays. You just have to be able to show your young players the basic mechanics. You also must have sufficient knowledge of the game to be able to answer questions. If you don't have all the skills, be smart enough to ask for help. Look for an assistant who supplements your own abilities. As the kids get older and you move up the youth baseball ladder, your level of knowledge must also increase, from basic skills to execution with strategy.

JOHN SMOLTZ

Pitcher, Atlanta Braves

★ Cy Young Award, 1996
★ Four-time All-Star
★ Played in five World Series
★ World Series Champions, 1995
★ Post-season record: 12-4
★ Most Valuable Player in NL Championship
  Series, 1992
★ All-time Braves record for wins in one season:
  24 in 1996
★ Father of four

I started playing baseball when I was seven years old, but I always played other sports as well and didn't really think about specializing in baseball until I was a senior in high school. If fact, I was planning to play both basketball and baseball in college, but, then, the very day before classes were starting at Michigan State, I signed a baseball contract.

I always had great fun playing baseball as a kid. I guess the very best times we had were just going to the park, unsupervised, and playing ball. But I was also very fortunate to have had as my summer league coach a man named Carl Wagner, who coached me every year from fifth grade throughout my high school years.

Coach Wagner was definitely the most important person in my early development into a baseball player. I'm sure this was true for a lot of other kids, too. He had a super attitude, always positive, he spent whatever time it took, and he was a great teacher. We won a lot of championships for Coach Wagner, but he never let it go to our heads. His great lesson was, "When you think you have arrived, you are in trouble."

My parents never pushed me toward baseball or other sports. In fact, I pushed harder than they did. But when they realized I really wanted to play, they gave me every opportunity to pursue it. My dad worked two jobs and traveled a lot, but no matter what his schedule was, he was always there to watch me play. I really appreciated that.

My advice to parents is to try to see baseball through your kid's eyes. Try to understand what he wants to get out of the game and support that. Parents sometimes have a hard time understanding that what the kid wants is not always going to be what the parents want.

Parents also don't always understand that they can't teach *desire*. So they push, when they just need to be patient. It's hard to be patient, I know, but pushing can backfire.

And when it comes to trying to figure out what kind of player their child is, parents need to look through the coach's eyes. There's no way parents are going to be objective. They really need someone else to evaluate their kid's ability and potential.

To coaches, I would mostly like to express my appreciation. I am amazed at how much time and energy these volunteers give to youth baseball. The only explanation for it is that they really love the game and they really want to make a difference in kids' lives.

I would also like to remind them: When you think you are appreciated the least, you will be appreciated the most.

As for advice, I would hope that coaches would go beyond teaching baseball skills and help their players become better people.

Also, I'd like to see coaches teach that it's okay to be a nerd – that you can be a nerd and still get ahead.

Finally, I think it was important that both my coach and my parents made sure that I kept winning in perspective. I certainly always played my hardest, tried my best to win, and we won a lot of games. But that's not what was being pushed.

Clearly, in many programs winning is overemphasized, as are individual awards and recognition like All-Star selections. It is ridiculous to be selecting All-Stars any earlier than age 12, if that. For one thing, the kids are already playing too many games, without the added pressure of All-Star games. And for another, the kids who don't make these teams get the message that they're not very good. That's a very poor message for coaches and programs to be sending.

II. BE A CARING PERSON

When I interview college and professional baseball players and coaches, I often pose the question, "What kind of person would you want working with your child in baseball?" Their answers always begin with, "Someone who loves kids, who enjoys being around kids, and someone who is there when kids need them." Sometimes it takes a little extra work to care every day. But as coaches you have to care every day! You are a symbol of what kids want to be. Caring also means being honest with both kids and their parents. Caring means having a plan, and helping everyone understand the plan, and making the parents a part of the plan. Caring means communicating regularly with parents, recognizing the positive things their kids do and talking with parents about things they can do at home to help their kids improve their skills.

III. BE A ROLE MODEL

Don't think for a minute that you are not supposed to be a role model. That may be the most important thing you have to do in the youth baseball environment. Kids see you during the good times and well as the bad times. They watch you discuss issues with other coaches and with parents. They learn something from you every day. They most certainly model their behavior on how they see you behave. You are in a position to have a tremendous impact on kids' attitudes toward competition, toward self-discipline, and toward developing a healthy definition of winning. How many hundreds of thousands of kids have wanted to be like their coach? Even an indifferent coach, on the technical level, can be a tremendous teacher about life. How many kids quit baseball because of their coach? I have friends whose children quit not only baseball but all other sports because of negative experiences with youth baseball coaches. My children have played baseball for several years with only one bad experience. But that coach was so bad he drove his own son out of the sport.

Credibility and respect are tremendous quali-
ties, and difficult to earn. Kids don't hand out the
accolades with reckless abandon. They watch, listen, and decide if you deserve their time and attention. Committing to being a positive role model
will get you where you and the kids need to go.

IV. LEARN SOMETHING EVERY DAY ABOUT KIDS

Yes, the coach can learn as much as the kids. Learn what pushes each youngster's motivation button. You'll find that most of your players are motivated not by you, but by the game, the field, the other kids, and the basic need we all have to compete.

On the field in front of you, you have an ongoing, real-life experiment in growth and development. When kids come to you to learn to play baseball or to refine their skills, they are in the process of developing their self-concept. What a fascinating thing to watch! What an important process to be a positive part of! Resist the temptation to spend most of your time with the most talented players. Not only will you risk damaging the self-concept of the less advanced player; you'll also deprive yourself of the pleasure of watching how quickly some of the beginning players can advance. Believe me, it is virtually impossible to predict how quickly and how well kids will develop baseball skills.

Learn about "critical learning periods" (which we also touched on in the *Tips for Parents* section). It's important to understand that kids mature physically, mentally, emotionally, and socially – but not all at the same rate. We often observe kids who are big, strong, and fast, who can throw and hit, but who are clearly not ready to cope with the mental stress of competition. If we put them in the wrong situation at the wrong time, we run the risk of losing them from not only baseball but other sports as well. Allow for differences in both skill and attitude. Don't force participation. Let it happen.

And remember: spend time with every player. This will not only increase your knowledge about kids; it's also your best opportunity to encourage them to stay with the game and become the best athletes they can.

V. CHECK YOUR OWN ATTITUDE BEFORE TRYING TO SHAPE KIDS' ATTITUDES

Never take a bad attitude to the practice field or to the game. Kids don't care whether or not you made the big sale, or that it was too hot outside to work, or that your boss yelled at you. Kids just want to play baseball. If you are tense or negative, just sit in the car a couple of extra minutes and think about what you are able to give kids in the next hour or two. Make some notes about what you want to accomplish today and take the list to the field so that you stay focused on what's important, especially if you begin to have a relapse during a frustrating part of practice. I have professional baseball clients who do this exercise every day. They keep the list in their pocket to review during adversity. It pulls you back on track.

Kids' attitudes will usually be positive unless they sense that you are having a bad day. There's no question that your attitude causes the entire environment to be positive or negative. You should be able to smile when practice or the game is over. You want to be certain that the kids had fun, and, just as important, they need to know that you had fun.

VI. EXPECT GOOD THINGS TO HAPPEN EVERY DAY

It is human nature to look for and correct mistakes. We do it in life, on our jobs, and in sports. In fact, our mistakes generally command more attention than do our achievements. The unfortunate consequence is that we spend a large percentage of our days trying to not fail. We begin to play to *not lose*. We hope to not fail, assuming that if we don't fail, then success will be a natural consequence. Not true! Attempting to avoid failure seldom results in success. Expecting to succeed at the very least increases your probability of accomplishing your goals.

Coaches too often take this "try to not fail" attitude to the baseball field. We talk more to kids about not missing the ball than we talk about catching or hitting the ball. We talk about avoiding bad swings more than talking about having good swings. We must create expectations of success for children. If you do nothing but engender in kids a sense of positive expectations, you do a tremendous service.

"If they hit it to you, don't miss it! If you catch

it, don't throw it to the wrong base!" It's not hard to see that this kind of instruction can increase a kid's tension to an unhealthy level, making failure more likely than success. I'm not suggesting that you should not recognize and correct mistakes. We obviously get better by learning to do things correctly. But kids need encouragement along with correction.

A good rule – and a very old one – is the "sandwich" approach. When you see mistakes: (1) open with a positive comment about something the player did well; (2) offer the appropriate criticism; and (3) conclude with some positive encouragement. The worst and probably the most frequently heard comment by coaches is, "That's wrong, let's do it again!" Remember, when you ask kids to do something, let them hear the instructions, let them touch the ball or bat, and let them practice the skill. And above all, never miss an opportunity to give positive reinforcement.

Basically, your expectations shape the performance of kids in baseball. Expect good things, and get good things. Expect negative things, and get negative things.

VII. LEARN HOW TO MOTIVATE YOUR KIDS

You don't have to be a Knute Rockne. Your kids are likely to have plenty of motivation already, and your task will probably be simply channeling their boundless energy. However, you do need to understand that different kids will respond to different keys.

What motivates one player may very well have no effect the next. In fact, when your motivational effort outweighs the players' need for external motivation, performance can actually suffer. At this age, children are eager to move, to achieve, and most of all, to be a part of a group. This is good, but you must understand why kids are on your team in the first place. Their parents may have actually "volunteered" for them; their peers may have exerted pressure on them; or they may be there just because they need to support their self-concept. Once they are there, how can you convince them to put their positive energy into participating?

The best motivator is action. Make sure that all kids are doing something all the time. Keep them busy. Make the drills fun, perhaps by changing the routine. Take short breaks to talk about what's going on. Make sure that all kids are in fair, competitive situations. If kids get too excited, give them a break to calm down, but let the kids perform at as high an emotional level as they can control.

Whatever kind of motivation you're using, remember that timing is critical. To be effective, motivation must occur when the young player will most benefit from a feeling of recognition, belonging, or success.

I would caution against using external rewards for performance with the young players. Encourage kids to play for the intrinsic reasons – because they want to play, because it's fun. When you introduce a reward system, you run the risk of having kids begin to play only when rewards are offered. I think, over the long term, that such things as game balls and All-Star recognition in T-ball are very negative. The time will come soon enough when kids will begin to recognize the potential for getting rewards from baseball.

Finally, *don't overmotivate*. Sometimes we coaches get so involved in the action that we lose track of our mission, which is to make baseball fun for kids. Sometimes our own excitement pushes the kids to an anxiety level that becomes unproductive. If we're too excited, too pumped, it's easy to forget who to throw to on a double-play, for example. It's the coach's job to help the kids channel that anxiety into positive, controlled energy – a worthy challenge, as we all know. The worst thing you can do is talk to your young players about how important a game is. Every game is important to them, just because they get to play.

VIII. KNOW HOW KIDS LEARN BASEBALL SKILLS

First a quick review of how our systems receive and process information. It's not unlike a computer: information in and information out. Kids receive information through several senses. They see what you have to offer. They hear what you are saying about what they see. And they touch whatever it is about which they are learning, a certain grip on the ball or a grip on the bat. Then they experience information from their muscles and joints about how to position their bodies to catch, throw, run, and hit. Every time you teach a skill, make sure that, if possible, every kid uses at least these four vehicles to receive important information so that they can fully process it.

Finally, analyze each skill so that you can teach the parts in the appropriate sequence. Kids need to learn each part before going to the next part. For example, in hitting, even though a youngster may go through the full motion, you need to emphasize different parts of the swing for him to master. The primary reason kids have so much trouble correcting mistakes is that we as coaches overload the system with corrections. Be specific and be patient.

IX. CONTINUE TO LEARN HOW TO TEACH BASEBALL

Just like the kids, coaches never stop learning. Be willing to attend clinics, to read, and to learn from each other. When I go to rookie camps for major league baseball, I see coaches teaching fundamentals, teaching kids to unlearn bad habits. You have a tremendous opportunity to teach kids correct skills, to set the stage for success. But you need to know the skills yourself. Remember: your challenge in youth baseball is that you may only have one chance to capture these kids and to get them excited about baseball.

Here are a couple of the current teaching theories:

⦿ Whole v. Part Learning: i.e., teaching a certain skill (say, hitting) as a whole or breaking it down into parts. As noted, for young kids I recommend teaching a skill like hitting in parts. In fact, the method called "progressive-part" teaching may be best. Using this technique, you start at the beginning of the skill and teach Part A before B, then combine A and B before C. When you complete the teaching, every kid will be

able to execute the entire skill more proficient-
ly. Obviously, the more complex the skill, the
more likely that you would use progressive-part
teaching.

◉ Massed v. Distributed Practice: i.e., how long you
practice without a break. I think with young kids
you need to use distributed practice. Practice for
10 or 15 minutes, take a break, then practice for
another 10 or 15 minutes before the next break.
The breaks give the players time to pull the
information together, to mentally rehearse
everything they learn. A related issue deals with
how long you stay at the field. Some youth
coaches keep kids at practice for over three
hours. I would maintain that at least two of those
hours are wasted.

You must teach kids baseball when they are
attentive, and when they can concentrate— in
other words, a very short period of time. As
skills improve, practices can go longer without
a break.

TERRY MULHOLLAND
Pitcher, Pittsburgh Pirates

★ 14 years in the Major Leagues
★ Played in two World Series
★ All-Star, 1993
★ Pitched no-hitter in 1990
★ Father of three

I played catch with my dad as early as I can remember and probably had started playing organized baseball by the age of seven. Everybody around played baseball. I had four younger brothers, and we all played.

I also played football up to my sophomore year in high school and basketball throughout high school, but baseball was always my main interest. To tell you the truth, I was already thinking about playing professional baseball when I was eight years old. I wasn't thinking about being a pitcher, though. I grew up playing first base and outfield. It wasn't until I was a freshman at Marietta College that I focused on pitching.

My parents were great – always eager to provide all five of us boys with sports experiences. Mom's department was transportation services; she got us where we needed to be all during the week. Dad, who also coached for a couple of years, was there every weekend, either playing with us or watching us play. They both wanted us to have fun and never encouraged us to think of winning as a life-or-death matter.

And we did have fun, great fun, and learned the important things that being on a team teaches you. I must say, though, that as a youngster I took the game a little too personally. I let little things bother me and was too easily upset, a problem I battled for a long time.

Two experiences helped me "adjust" my attitude.

The first happened one day in junior league ball when an older guy, in his sixties maybe, made a comment to me that I've never forgotten. This guy was a complete stranger who happened to watch me play, then came up and told me that I was a good player but that I was letting my head get in my way. I was capable of making great plays, he said, but I was making mistakes because of my head. He concluded by saying, "This is a game. You will win and you will lose."

The second happened when I was 15 and had to have knee surgery. I ended up with a staph infection and almost lost my leg. My temperature soared up to 106. I was so sick I lost 55 pounds and took a year to get my strength back. Man, that really put things in perspective – it put baseball in perspective. I discovered that losing a baseball game wasn't the end of the world. These two experiences did wonders for my demeanor.

The most important thing I would tell parents is, "Listen to your kids." If your children don't happen to like baseball, don't take it personally.

If your children do want to play baseball, my advice is to do a little homework on the team and the league. For example, do all the kids on the team get to play? Is the emphasis on enjoyment? Are winning and competition kept in proper perspective? These are some of the questions I'd want answers to before I signed my kid up.

My advice to coaches? MAKE IT FUN! After all, how can you expect kids to want to get good at the game if they're not having a good time?

Also, I think that coaches and teams and leagues need to rethink the All-Star concept. In the first place, baseball is supposed to be a *team* sport, and the kids need to be learning how to be teammates, not about being singled out for individual recognition. The All-Star thing seems to be more for the parents' benefit than the kids'.

True, the time comes when individual talent and achievement should be recognized, maybe beginning at about 13 or 14 years old. But we are starting way earlier than that, which I think is a bad idea. When kids 10 years old and younger are not picked for these teams, it says to them, "You are not good enough." They don't need to hear that.

How to deal with parents who get out of hand can be a tough question. But I think the solution is for the coach just to take them aside and have a long, hard talk. Maybe he can persuade them that yelling and making a scene is not doing their kid any good, that it just takes the fun out of the game. Maybe he can make them understand that sometimes the best thing is not to win.

It seems like parents have gotten brainwashed by the media into looking at baseball's income-earning potential. There are so many other things – more important things – for young players to take from baseball. Baseball's real value is in what it teaches about success and failure, about team membership, about self-discipline, about social skills.

As for handling players with discipline problems, again I think the key is priorities. The coach needs to communicate to the players and to their parents that –

⦿ His goal is to make the experience fun;

⦿ He will make sure that every kid plays;

⦿ And that anybody who doesn't plan to abide by his rules can go elsewhere.

If I were the coach, I would much rather have nine little boys playing hard as teammates – win or lose – than a bunch of kids looking for individual glory.

X. SET GOALS WITH KIDS

Too often we adults assume that we know what kids' goals are in baseball. We don't stop to realize that for the very young player, maybe the goal is to get dirty, or just to swing the bat, or to be a part of the team and get a uniform. I had a T-ball player who just dropped his glove in left field and went to the park to swing. As a coach, you must help the kids set their baseball goals, not their parents' goals, but their individual goals. Those goals need to be challenging, specific, and most importantly, attainable. At the same time, you can be encouraging your players to view sport as a rewarding, enjoyable experience – win or lose. So make sure the goals you set help the kids "enjoy the journey."

Review the goals weekly. If they are unrealistic, then change them. You might combine the individual goals and set team goals. This enables youngsters to see how their individual performances relate to the bigger picture.

XI. DECIDE HOW EVERYONE SHOULD PARTICIPATE

This question depends on the age of your players. With younger kids, up to 12 or 13 years old, participation should be a non-issue. Every player should play in every game. They learn by competing. Perhaps the real issue with these younger players is what position they should play. Be sure never to put a child in a position that might be unsafe. Some kids may not be comfortable in positions close to the action, and you must respect the child's feelings. Parents may pressure you to put their kids in at highly visible positions, but your major concern is the safety of the child and the building of self-concept – not the destruction of self-concept. One thing we may forget is that some kids are not ready to play key roles, but they are ready to have uniforms. To these kids, practice may be participation. At all costs avoid embarrassing kids.

When players get older in the youth sport programs, they begin to appreciate talent and better understand why they play or don't play. They begin to understand about team goals and about winning, not only the process but winning on the scoreboard. This is the age when parents, if uneducated about what you are trying to accomplish, can become a real problem. You need to tell parents on the first day what you plan to do about participation. They can then make a decision about leaving their kids with you or taking them to another league. I personally think that all kids should play in every game at least until they reach high school. You need to keep them in the program, not chase them away.

XII. PROVIDE A BROAD EXPERIENCE FOR EVERY PLAYER

I strongly support the idea of having kids play different positions during the course of a season. Too often we stereotype kids for positions (left-handers on first base, in the outfield, or pitch, etc.). Very few of the professional players whom we interviewed played their present position in youth baseball. Some pitchers didn't pitch until high school, some not until college, and a surprising number didn't pitch until they became professional players. To the greatest extent possible, kids need to play every position on the field. As they grow physically and their strength and flexibility change, they will naturally begin to play fewer positions. You may need to encourage kids to play different positions before they become comfortable in one spot and refuse to move around.

While you're at it, provide a broad experience in perceptual development as well as physical development.

⊛ Visual perception: Talk with young players about watching the ball, tracking the flight of the ball.

Talk with them about visually focusing on a specific thing as well as using their peripheral vision to see a much broader area during performance.

◉ Auditory perception: Teach your players to listen not only to your instructions, but to the "crack" of the bat, which gives them information about where the ball is going.

◉ Tactile perception: Make sure every kid has a ball. While you are demonstrating the grip, the kids need to grip the ball. This also holds true with catching and with gripping the bat while hitting.

◉ Kinesthetic awareness: This is simply becoming aware of where body parts are at all times. Let the kids run, jump, slide, and stretch whenever possible in order to improve their kinesthetic awareness.

Deepen their physical experience by continually exposing kids to activities that contribute to strength, endurance, balance, flexibility, agility, and coordination.

XIII. DEAL WITH YOUR EMOTIONS AND HELP KIDS DEAL WITH THEIR EMOTIONS

Emotions always run high during youth league baseball games for coaches, parents, and kids. A competitive environment seems to trigger emotions even in those who don't ordinarily compete. Most problems in the youth baseball programs are, in fact, caused by emotions that have gone over the edge. Emotions either help you to become better or they become detriments to performance. They don't lie dormant in your system. Your job as a coach is twofold: first, to teach kids how to use their emotions in a positive way in order to play better *and* to enjoy the game; and, second, to help parents understand how to show their emotions in a positive way that supports all the players on both teams. If parents feel themselves going over the edge, they need to walk away and take a deep breath and think about why they are there.

We know that there is an optimal level of emotion for best performance. Being too relaxed can be as detrimental as being too emotional. On a 1-10 scale, the ideal emotional register is probably at 6 or 7. You are responsible for helping the kids get to that ideal level, and helping them get back under control if they get too far beyond it. One technique is to have them practice taking a deep breath and mentally seeing what they want to do next. They are not relaxing; they are just getting under control emotionally. If they get too emotional about losing a game, they should take a moment to think about some specific things they did well during the game. Then look forward to the next game.

Now for your emotions. You must show your young players positive emotional control. If you get caught up in the heat of the battle, you need to step back and think about why you are coaching. This environment has nothing to do with your job, it has nothing to do with your home life; it has everything to do with these young people, with providing for them a positive experience. Your basic assumption should be that every player is trying as hard as he can, and that human nature dictates that we are going to make mistakes, and that someone will benefit and someone will not. That's one of the things that make baseball so exciting. If your team wins, there's another day. If your team loses, there's another day.

XIV. TEACH KIDS TO APPRECIATE WINNING . . . AND WINNING EFFORTS

It's interesting: in our talks with coaches and parents, both groups agree that winning is secondary to participation. Yet both groups behave at games as if winning were the savior of youth and of themselves. We really need to understand that, especially with the youngsters, "winning" goes far beyond the scoreboard. I will never forget when I coached T-ball. To avoid the win-at-all-costs attitude, we decided that no score would be kept. We would play for one hour and go home. The excitement was there, kids learned basic skills, and everyone played, and everyone had fun. One problem: We had two games protested by parents. *They wanted the score kept.*

It's very simple. In youth baseball winning has to do with effort. If I play hard – regardless of the score – I am a winner, not a loser. Playing hard every day is winning; developing self-discipline is winning; developing a healthy, positive attitude toward yourself and toward baseball is winning. Knowing you gave everything you had is winning.

The winning coach is not the one whose team goes 10-0 and nobody plays the next year. The winning coach is the one whose team is 5-5 and everybody plays next year.

As a coach you must look for the things – beyond the scoreboard – that give you a feeling of fulfillment. Look for fulfillment in the kids' effort and enjoyment, in the parents' comments and support, and in the number of players from your team who plan to play next season.

DR. JOE CHANDLER

Orthopedic Surgeon

★ 14 years in Sports Medicine
★ Attending physician to the Atlanta Braves
★ Specialist in throwing-arm injuries among young players

Parents, coaches, players – please listen up. *We are seeing way too many arm injuries among players high school age and younger!*

Why? Because young players are throwing too many breaking pitches too early, and often with incorrect mechanics.

The solution? Prevention, even if it means rule changes.

My years of research into throwing-arm injuries have led me to a number of conclusions, which I would like to share even though they are often at odds with what coaches and parents want to hear:

◉ First and foremost, kids are throwing too many pitches too early; and, more specifically, they are throwing too many breaking pitches too early.

- We must protect young arms. Eight to 10 years old is not necessarily too young to start pitching, as long as it's fast balls only. It's generally safe to start working on the change-up at age 11 or 12.

- For kids of average size, age 14 is the optimum time to begin throwing breaking balls, if your mechanics are sound. Note: Many young players try to learn breaking pitches by using the slider motion, which almost certainly will hurt their arms.

- Among 30 major league pitchers interviewed, the average age at which they began to throw breaking pitches was 14.6 years old. Among 70 minor league pitchers interviewed, the average age was just under 14 years.

- That said, it's important to consider a young player's physical maturity as well as his age. In fact, research shows that for kids who are strong enough, the curve ball – if thrown correctly –

will cause less arm stress than the fastball.

- In mandating how many pitches young players can pitch during a game, we need to look at pitch count rather than number of innings. For example, pitchers 12 and younger should be limited to 50 pitches, regardless of inning.

- Understandably, young pitchers fall in love with the breaking ball. Their use of these pitches needs to be carefully monitored. In one 11-year-olds' tournament we researched, 50 percent of the pitchers threw breaking balls. In a tournament for 12-year-olds, every pitcher was throwing breaking balls. This is extremely unwise.

- SURGERY WILL NOT CURE ALL PROBLEMS! How many young pitchers continue to be successful after "Tommy John" surgery? The answer is: not many.

- So-called "traveling teams," in general, exert too much pressure physically on young players. The level of competition is tempting, but players' longevity in the sport can be significantly diminished.

⊚ Young athletes should be encouraged to play several sports, in order to enhance their overall physical development.

To conclude on a more general note: the No. 1 priority in youth baseball should be to have fun. The game is not, and should not be considered, major league preparation. In addition to having a good time, we need to stress good sportsmanship and overall physical fitness. Parents should look for programs where these priorities are paramount.

XV. TEACH KIDS HOW TO RECOVER FROM ADVERSITY

Adversity is a part of life whether you are a five-year-old baseball player or a 50-year-old professional person. The question is how to deal with it. Some kids get rattled by adversity and begin to let the fear of failure dictate their play. Others try to avoid the whole issue by never trying to get better; they understand that improved skills will lead to higher expectations and, at some point, disappointment.

The answer in both cases is learning to recover quickly from adversity. Here's the key: Teach your players to mentally store the good things they do – every tough play they make, every big hit. Then when they fail – or fear that they might fail – all they have to do is mentally replay some of those good things. This exercise – as simple as rerunning a video tape – will get the kids' emotions on a positive track and give them an image of what they want to accomplish.

As the coach, your job is to focus on the recovery, not on the adversity.

XVI. EDUCATE PARENTS IF YOU HOPE TO BE SUCCESSFUL

Educating your players' parents is probably the very first thing you need to worry about. Without their support, you will be fighting an uphill battle with the kids. When I start a program with a professional baseball player, I first spend time with his coach. I need a support system in place for the program to work. I need daily reinforcement when I am not with the player. The key is to get parents involved on the field. When the kids start throwing, let the parents throw with them. And share with the parents your plans for teaching their child, for making the environment fun, and for helping the child develop skills they can use outside baseball. Who knows? Maybe this will carry over to more time together at home.

While you're educating the parents, don't forget to compliment them. Compliment them for their positive reinforcement. Compliment them for their attendance. Compliment them for transporting the kids to and from practice and games.

And most important, deliver on your promises

to them every day. Remember that the bottom line is that everyone experience positive things in youth baseball. Remember that individuals don't win and lose, teams win and lose, and that your team includes you, your family, your players, and their families. Spend the time to keep everyone on the right track.

COACHES' QUESTIONS & ANSWERS

Following are some of the questions most frequently asked by coaches in clinics. The list is by no means inclusive, but it may include some that have occurred to you in your challenging role as a youth baseball coach.

1. On a list of priorities, where is "winning"?

We have found that winning, in the sense of outscoring your opponent, begins to become very important at age 11 or 12. But with the younger kids, winning has a much broader definition. Trying hard is winning. Showing good sportsmanship is winning. Learning how to play on a team is winning. Learning self-discipline is winning.

You have to help kids – and especially their parents – understand the importance of the "journey." Remember the study that showed more than 80 percent of five- and six-year-olds did not know if they won or lost after the game was over. Their focus was where it should be – on having fun.

Make no mistake: The older kids need to understand how to win *and* how to lose. In fact, it's through losing that they learn how to recover from adversity, a skill that will help them throughout life. I worked with a professional player several years ago who had never lost. He had always been better than other kids in his neighborhood and throughout high school. The first time he was defeated in professional baseball, he could not deal with the adversity. He lasted less than one summer – a shame and a waste of talent. You learn more ways to win by losing on occasion.

Never downgrade the importance of playing to win. Just change your definition as your players move up.

2. Following up Question 1, should the goals of youth baseball be different at each age level?

Yes. For the very young (5-8), the score doesn't matter. Participation is important, along with learning to run, to swing the bat, to throw, and hopefully to catch. And attitude is important: having fun, enjoying peer approval, and developing self-image.

For the next group (9-12), competition becomes

more intense, and winning is beginning to be emphasized. Kids are more peer conscious and want to perform well. Now we begin to work on cognitive skills, self-discipline, strategies for winning, responsibility, and social interaction.

For the older group (13-15), the fundamentals should be in place. Now our goals are honing skills, mastering strategy, and deepening game knowledge. Decision-making increases, accountability becomes more important, and kids begin to accept the consequences of their actions.

3. What is my goal as a coach?

Aside from enabling kids to achieve the goals outlined above, you have one primary goal: to help the players have fun playing baseball and to have fun yourself. You'll have a good chance of achieving this goal if you have a burning desire to be a good teacher, and if you genuinely care about each player, not only as an athlete but as a person.

RON POLK
Coach, University of Georgia

---

* ★ 33 years of coaching at university level
* ★ Conducts clinics for coaches worldwide
* ★ Coached seven international tours with the USA baseball program
* ★ Assistant coach, U.S. Olympic team, 1988 and 1996
* ★ Coach, U.S. Pan Am team, 1991

Kids today, I think, feel pressured into specializing too early. They choose one sport too early, and one position in that sport too early. Kids should play all sports, or as many as possible. As youngsters in baseball, they need to get back to playing for fun with or without a coach or uniforms. It seems to me that kids don't play as much on their own these days because of all the other distractions available to them. As a result, we are losing too many kids from all sports.

So when our kids are interested in getting into a youth baseball program, we need to do everything we can to make the experience a good one. That starts with making sure they're in the right environment.

Here are some of the most important things parents should consider when trying to find the right program, especially at the younger levels:

● Who is the coach?

● Will the kids enjoy the game with this coach?

● Will the experience be fun and positive?

● Will the kids learn the basics, will they learn how to play the game?

When the players get a little older, at 15 to 17 years old, parents also need to consider how many games they are playing, how much travel is involved, and what types of transportation.

My advice for coaches? Simple:

⊙ Teach the fundamentals correctly – how to throw, how to field the ball, how to hit, how to run.

⊙ Let the kids play multiple positions.

⊙ Teach the kids to let themselves play the game. Don't try to force everything.

⊙ Help the kids learn about competition, but without too much emphasis on winning. The emphasis should be on playing the game.

The most important thing kids should be getting out of youth baseball, without a doubt, is fun. They should enjoy playing the game. Here's a story to illustrate my point. After two teams had completed a game, the coaches decided to play another couple of innings. One of the younger kids said, "Yeah, we played one game for the scoreboard, now let's play a game for fun!"

Of course, kids should also learn from youth baseball important lessons about teamwork, and about how to handle both success and failure. And they will learn those things, if they're having enough fun to stick around.

4. Should I coach my own child?

Review the discussion of this question in the "Tips for Parents" section. The situation to avoid here is when your expectations become unrealistic, and you end up coaching your child at breakfast, lunch, and dinner, as well as on the way to and from practice. Carefully examine your priorities for your child. If you expect too much, then be honest enough to not coach him.

5. When should I have kids specialize in one position?

Never! Let the young kids play everywhere. When they get to be teenagers, they will be able to make a choice. Look at all the professionals who are changing positions late in their careers. There's a successful major league pitcher today who never pitched until late in his minor league career. Several players have moved to the outfield after a career in the infield. One all-star second baseman was an all-star catcher. These players are able to move around because they had a broad background as youngsters, which helped them to become better athletes.

6. How can I attend to safety in the baseball environment?

My opinion is that every league should have a trainer at every park. But in the meantime, attend clinics on athletic training, prevention, and emergency care of injuries. Make sure your players' equipment is in good shape. And if there is an injury, do only what you are qualified to do.

One recent safety innovation is the chest protector that's now available. It's not required for youngsters, but perhaps should be. It fits around the chest and molds itself to the shape of the player. It's comfortable, does not restrict movement, and protects the chest area very effectively. I know several professional players who won't let their youngsters play without the protector. Review the serious and even fatal injury reports and you will discover that most of them occur as a result of being hit in the chest by a thrown or batted ball. We protect the face with equipment. Why not protect the very vulnerable chest as well?

But back to what you should do: Be sure to inspect the field every day, removing any potentially dangerous objects. Never stop reminding your players to be careful around the batting area. Perhaps the most important thing is to teach kids to pay attention *all the time.*

7. Should every kid participate?

Most leagues require participation. I really like the rule that allows kids to bat even when they're not playing in the field. Young players play the game so they can swing the bat. My only hesitation over required participation is the safety issue. You don't want to place your kids in a situation where they might get hurt. There is a reason that younger kids are put in right field even when they cannot catch. Out there they can usually get out of the way of the ball before it gets to them, then chase it down. They can even spend some time catching grasshoppers when things are slow. Not a bad thing. They are in the game; they are playing.

As kids get older, the participation rule gets a bit more complicated. Kids begin to realize that in order to win, the better players need to play. This should act as motivation for the lesser-skilled kids to become better. Some kids will sit on the bench if the team wins and be perfectly happy. Most kids, however, have stated in surveys that they had rather play on a losing team than sit on the bench on a winning team. And every kid that wants to play should get the opportunity.

8. How do you deal with rowdy parents?

If you are doing what you should be doing, most parents are supportive. There will, however, be a few who either don't want to be there or else are there only to live vicariously through their youngster. These parents can very difficult, sometimes intolerable.

I always tried to do two things: First, I explained to the parents what we were doing and why we were there, and I begged for their help and support. Second, I tried to involve every parent in the teaching process, to have them on the field whenever possible.

With a hopelessly disruptive parent, you might try what I tried: put him on one of the bases as an assistant coach. If nothing else, he'll probably discover that baseball is a very difficult game to play. If that doesn't work, you might have to ask the parent to go sit in his car and think about what he wants his child to get out of the youth baseball experience.

9. How do I deal with players who don't want to be there?

First, talk with the child and get a feel for what he is interested in. If he likes to compete – just not in baseball – structure some basic skills competition that might get him involved. Perhaps he has simply not played baseball and is reluctant to look like a rookie while his peers are watching.

Next, talk with his parents and try to establish whose idea it was to play baseball. If it was the parents' idea, maybe they need to explore other activities for the child until he shows an interest in baseball. Sometimes we forget that youth baseball was established for kids, not for adults and not for baby-sitting.

10. What about after-game awards?

I think most kids play the game initially for the treat afterwards. Spending an hour playing baseball is a small price to pay in exchange for a hot dog and a Coke.

As for awards, though, I think they are a bad idea. They're too subjective, they mean more to parents than to kids, and they cause unnecessary conflict and jealousy. What does a game ball mean to a young child whose real reward is simply life after the game? What does being an All-Star mean to a six-year-old?

11. What about year-round baseball?

This is another bad idea for the most part. Kids need a well-rounded experience in sports: baseball during baseball season and other sports during other seasons. Younger kids, especially, are far from ready to choose just one sport. As they get older, perhaps after 14, they may have had enough experience to specialize. But, even then, I hate to see high school kids who are good in two or more sports drop everything for one sport. Remember: there are no guarantees.

So many of the athletes I've worked with over the years played at least two sports through high

school. In fact, one major leaguer never played
baseball until his senior year in college. He was a
basketball player, but decided to play baseball in
the spring of his senior year to have something to
do. Three years later he was a relief pitcher for a
major league team. Year-round baseball takes
these experiences away from kids. But if they do
decide to play only baseball after trying other
sports, just make sure it's their choice, not yours
and not their parents'.

Part 3
Tips for Athletes

First, a question: Do you like to play baseball? If the answer is yes, if you *want to play,* then go ahead and make a commitment to becoming the best baseball player you can be. How? Well, here are a few starting points:

⦿ Listen to your coach.

⦿ Work hard to master baseball's basic skills.

⦿ Learn the real meaning of winning.

⊙ Let baseball teach you how to recover from
   adversity.

⊙ And, most important, have fun out there every
   day.

The following pages elaborate on these tips. Take a
look at them. Keep them by you. They may prove
helpful – especially when things are not going just
right for you on any given day.

I. PLAY BASEBALL BECAUSE YOU LIKE IT

Think about all the things you do just because you like to do them – things like snacking on your favorite food, playing video games, and riding your bike. When for some reason you *can't* do these things, you get upset, right? This is how you should feel about baseball. You should play because you like to, and you should be disappointed when you can't play.

Fun is the name of the game. If it's no fun, then let it go. Not wanting to play baseball does not make you a bad person. Maybe this isn't the right time for you; maybe you'll play later. Maybe not. But the thing is, playing when you don't enjoy it could turn you against all sports.

You might work hard at it, practice long hours, and even lose some games, but it should still be fun. Of course, it's much easier if the environment is fun. Sometimes you have to remind your parents and coaches that it's just a game after all.

II. SET GOALS FOR WHAT YOU WANT TO ACCOMPLISH DURING THE BASEBALL SEASON

Tell the coach that you want to set some personal goals, goals for you. You may want your parents to help, but be sure your coach and parents understand what you mean – what kind of goals you want. Make your goals specific enough so that you can know clearly whether you have achieved them. Make them difficult, challenging. The only way you get better at the game is to stretch your talent every day. Try to do more every day than you did the day before.

At the same time, make sure your goals are attainable. It is better to reach your goals and then move them higher than to realize that you can't achieve them and then have to lower them. Achieving goals helps you develop a better self-concept, as well as develop self-discipline. Let me suggest some goals you can start working on today.

A. Be in the best physical condition possible: Be able to play hard the whole game. Be able to run when others are tired; be able to run when you are tired. But give yourself time to improve your physical condition, and don't expect it to happen in a day, a week, or a month. It is an ongoing process.

B. Be in the best mental condition possible: Have a positive mental attitude about baseball. Have confidence in yourself. Confidence comes with success – not necessarily winning on the scoreboard but executing well consistently. You will make most of your mistakes when you are tired mentally, so learn how to think when you are tired, how to react mentally. Be able to make quick decisions.

C. Learn every skill in baseball: You don't have to be able to do all of them well, but you must know how to execute them. By attempting all the skills and all the positions, you learn greater respect for what others do well, and you also learn respect for your own talents. Kids are not born to play baseball or any other sport. You have to learn one skill at a time until you can play the game.

D. Learn your role on the team: Learn to be a good follower, a good team player, as well as a leader

when you need to be a leader. No matter what role
you play on the team, walk away every day with
the satisfaction that you did everything you could
do to help the team.

III. UNDERSTAND WINNING

First of all, winning in your own mind should not depend on the score on the board during the game. No matter what the final score, you should evaluate winning personally by what you were able to achieve during the game, your execution of skills, your decisions. Achievement, or "winning," may have been a good hit, a good catch, or a good throw. Maybe you learned something about your teammates. Maybe you got to know members of the other team. And, who knows, maybe you got to know yourself better. All these things are wins for you. If you work hard every minute of every practice and every game, you do not lose. The wins are not always obvious, but they are there.

Outscoring your opponent will get more important as you get older. That's part of the natural progression from the time you start at five or six years old to when you are really taking the game seriously at 14 or 15 years old. Being on the field and wearing a uniform is everything for you when you start, but playing well and playing to win will become the primary goal in good time. Regardless

of the age or level of play, however, the one con-
stant over time is the process. Be sure to enjoy the
process year after year.

Remember, also, that you don't have to be a
"star" to be a winner. Teams win because of team
effort. If you are not the "star," be happy in knowing that there would be no star without your help.
Be happy to play.

IV. LOOK FORWARD TO COMPETITION IN BASEBALL

Don't be reluctant to be competitive. Competition is a part of life, and one of the good things about baseball is that it provides an environment for keen and healthy competition.

In fact, after a game, you should feel good about knowing that you competed hard, that you competed fairly, and that you will be ready to compete the next time the opportunity comes. If you have this feeling after every game, regardless of the score and regardless of the amount of time you played, your coach, parents, and friends will recognize, respect, and be inspired by your effort.

V. LOOK FORWARD TO ACCEPTING THE CHALLENGES OFFERED IN BASEBALL

Accepting the challenges baseball offers will help you develop mentally and physically. You will improve your skills, which will make you feel good about yourself. You will learn to handle pressure – from your coaches, parents, and mostly from yourself. Here are three fundamental challenges for you to take on:

A. Listen to your coach. If you don't understand, ask questions. Don't be shy; you should be eager to learn.

B. Work hard at every practice. Always go home with a feeling that you gave it all you had. Know that you tried to do everything the right way.

C. After you learn to play, practice the skills in your mind. Mental practice is what makes the good players better.

VI. ENCOURAGE YOUR PARENTS TO WATCH YOU PRACTICE AND PLAY

It may be that they want to watch, but they are afraid they will make you nervous. If you practice with them around, then you will play games better when they are around. Sometimes, they just need to be asked.

If they observe how and what your coaches are teaching, then the chances are good that your parents will practice with you at home. Don't be upset if your parents don't know how to play baseball. Maybe they didn't get to play when they were growing up. Take the opportunity to learn together.

CHUCK KNOBLAUCH

Second Baseman, New York Yankees

★ AL Rookie of the Year, 1991
★ Four-time All-Star
★ Two-time Silver Slugger
★ Gold Glove, 1997
★ 10 years in major leagues

I started playing baseball when I was very young, probably about five years old. The coaches threw underhand, and I was in the "Tadpole League." My dad was a high school coach, though, so we played all the time. He would hit to me, let me bat, and throw with me.

I also played basketball and football up through my freshman year in high school, but starting with sophomore year I played only baseball. Actually, baseball was probably always my first choice, because I could feel myself getting better all the time.

I was always a shortstop – all the way through youth baseball and high school. I was even drafted as a shortstop in 1989. The first time I ever played second base was in a big-league training game my second year in the majors. Boy, was I nervous! I've been a second baseman ever since.

I'd say the most significant person in my development as a baseball player was my dad. Since he was the high school coach, he couldn't come to many of my games, but he always played the game with me; he taught me how to play. Also, I hung out with him at the high school all the time. But really, I got great support from both my parents, and my mom was always at my games.

Youth baseball was a great experience for me. I had great fun playing, and at the same time I could feel myself getting better, which made me want to keep playing.

The most important thing I learned was also the hardest thing to learn: that you can't win every time. I used to get so upset at losing. I was always a good competitor, and it was just very hard for me to accept losing. Baseball will eventually teach you, though.

★

My advice to parents is if your kids enjoy baseball, or any sport, give them all the encouragement you can. More specifically, if you're trying to find the right program for your child, I suggest, first, that you find out who's running the program, and, second, try to pick a program where kids are in fair situations. In my own experience, my parents took me out of one league and put me in another at age 13 so that the competition would be fair. That made my transition to the next level much easier.

As for coaches, the most important thing is to always be positive with the kids. A pat on the back can do wonders, and nobody likes being yelled at.

It's funny how vividly we remember the negative experiences. For the most part, my coaches were good, but I had one "yeller," really obnoxious. I'll never forget him. The ones you don't remember as well were probably doing a great job.

VII. EXPECT GOOD THINGS TO HAPPEN

Take it from me: If you expect to play well, you will play better. If you expect to play poorly, then you will play poorly. How many times have you gone to bat thinking, "I hope I don't strike out!" Most of the time the result will be a strikeout. Expect to hit the ball, expect to catch the ball, expect to throw the ball well, and expect to have a good time.

This attitude is harder to achieve than you might think. Your coach probably tells you constantly what *not* to do. And, as a result, we spend a great deal of time trying to not fail. If you play to win, there are no guarantees, but the chances of success increase dramatically. You will be amazed how many things will go well when you expect them to go well.

VIII.   LEARN TO RECOVER FROM ADVERSITY

Of course, the good things you expect to happen are not going to happen every time. You will have some bad days. You will lose some games. You will make an error every now and then. You will strike out with guys in scoring position.

To learn how to get over it, to recover from adversity, is one of the most important things baseball teaches. And it's not hard to learn. It begins with a fundamental lesson: What you just did is not the important thing. The important thing is what you are going to do. The secret is to file away the images of the times you did it right – got the hit, made the play – and call them up when you need them. Picture them vividly. Dwell on them. This is how to prepare to do the next thing right. This is how to recover.

IX. PLAY BASEBALL

When I was growing up, we played baseball almost every day. It was not always well organized, but there were two teams and we played until we got tired. We didn't have bats and baseballs. We used broomsticks and socks rolled up and taped together. If you hit the sock over the house, that was a home run. Nobody ever struck out. You batted until you hit the sock.

When it came time to play organized baseball with coaches and real bats and real baseballs and gloves, I wasn't sure I wanted to. I didn't know if playing by the rules would take the fun out of the game. But now, long after that first "organized" game, I look back at all the fun we had, and at all the friends I made, and at all the lessons I learned that have stayed with me to this day:

◉ I learned the correct way to play.

◉ I learned to assume a role on a team.

- I learned how and when to lead, and how and when to depend on others.

- I learned how to recover when things didn't go right.

When I look at my experiences and try to come up with a key point for you to remember, I keep recalling the advice I took from a professional player when I was 11 years old. He simply said, "Play baseball!"

When you are winning some games and losing some games, you must always remember that playing is what it's all about, that trying as hard as you can is your objective, that being proud of what you can do is most important. Don't play for rewards. Don't play because someone else plays. Don't play because parents or coaches force you to play. Play because you like it.

One last thing to remember, though, is that baseball is not the most important thing in your life. It can be a great part of your life, but it is only one part, another place to learn about yourself.

ATHLETES' QUESTIONS & ANSWERS

1. I'm 12 years old. Should I drop my other sports and play only baseball?

No! Every day I see young athletes specializing in one sport, and I find it very discouraging. You can never get too many experiences in sport. Different sports give you different skills that improve your balance, speed, quickness, strength, and endurance. Earliness is not the important thing. Timeliness is what matters. You have plenty of time to specialize. Two all-star baseball players I've worked with never played baseball until they were 17 or 18 years old. One was drafted by professional hockey but chose baseball. The other was recruited by over 50 universities to play basketball but chose baseball. Another all-star baseball player did not specialize in baseball until he had been an all-star professional football player. Tell your parents that you want to play lots of sports. If your youth coach wants you to specialize, then ask to change coaches. If baseball is your sport, you will naturally drop the other sports when the time is right.

2. When should I start switch-hitting?

First, I need to know whose idea it is for you to switch-hit. If you are comfortable, try it anytime. Remember, at an early age you are more apt to stay with the things that make you feel successful. Switch-hitting is not easy. If you try it, don't get discouraged. Be patient. You will do much better if it is your idea. If you have a lot of speed but not much power and are a right-handed hitter, then you might want to switch-hit to take advantage of standing on the left side of the plate – where you're that much closer to first base.

3. When should I start pitching?

You can pitch anytime, but there are some critical things you need to know. First, learn the correct mechanics of pitching so that you will not injure your arm or shoulder. Never practice unsupervised. Second, don't specialize in pitching at an early age. Play several positions. Many major league pitchers did not pitch until they were in their late teens or twenties. Third, don't pitch if your arm hurts. Coaches should know this, but sometimes they are too preoccupied with winning games. Pay close attention to the league rules regarding how many innings you can pitch in a week. If the league rule is seven innings per week and you play on two teams, that does not mean you can pitch 14 innings. That means seven total innings for thc wcck.

Perhaps the real issue is not when to pitch, but when to start throwing different pitches. I really hate seeing kids that are not even 10 years old throwing breaking pitches. Sure they will be successful, because hitters that age can't hit straight pitches, much less breaking pitches. The real problem is the stress on your young arm of throwing these pitches. Major league scouts tell me that they look for kids who have a strong arm and can throw strikes. You can learn breaking pitches later, much later. You have to think about developing your strength over the long term. What good is it for you to be the best pitcher from six years old to 14 years old and not be able to throw the ball across the room without pain after 14?

4. I know older kids who take supplements for strength and weight gain. Should I take something to help me get as big and strong as these kids?

Absolutely not! There is no justification for taking any type of drug to help you play better. Your body is still developing, and your growth should be natural. Many athletes who took supplements as professionals have tremendous health problems. Some feel that the supplements cut their careers short. Good nutrition and exercise are the keys to healthy growth and development.

5. I get really nervous before games. What can I do?

Try to figure out why you are nervous. If you are nervous because you want to get started, that is perfectly natural. If you are nervous because you feel that you are not ready to compete, then you need to examine your preparation methods. If you have not worked hard in practice, then you should be worried. The remedy for that is to have a practice plan and execute that plan every day.

Most of the time, pre-game nervousness is a

good thing. It simply means that you are anxious to show what you can do. I know one professional baseball player who got physically sick before every game (yes, 162 games), yet he was an exceptionally good player. Just take a deep breath and try to mentally picture yourself playing the game, perhaps hitting the ball or throwing the ball. When the game starts, repeat this process just before you hit, or just before an inning starts on defense. When you get into the game itself, your anxiety will go down significantly. After the game, you might find that you get nervous again. That is also natural. Again, just take a deep breath and think about some things you did well in the game.

Remember: Emotion is a tremendous asset. The rule is, "Play every day at as high an emotional level as you can control." As you get older and better at baseball, you can use your emotions to your advantage.

6. When I play really well, everyone congratulates me. Then I begin to make a lot of mistakes. Why?

You may be experiencing fear of success. It sounds

strange, but there are plenty of reasons for people to be afraid to succeed. Once you succeed, more is expected of you. You become more accountable. You are asked to take on more responsibility. Sometimes these changes come before we are ready for them, and they make us uneasy. So the alternative is to play okay, make a few mistakes, avoid being the star, and stay comfortable.

A better plan is to not get discouraged and to keep playing hard. As you play more, you will get comfortable with the attention off the field. And don't forget that visualization; when it's time to make the play, mentally see yourself performing well. Gradually you'll get comfortable with success.

7. My coach scares me. I'm afraid to make a mistake. Should I quit the game?

Don't quit baseball. But maybe you need a new coach. First, though, talk with the coach and explain how you feel. Maybe, with your help, he will come to understand that each child should be treated differently, both in how to offer positive reinforcement and how to correct mistakes. The last thing he should be doing is making his players uncomfortable. He may be beyond help, but honest communication with him can't hurt.

8. My dad keeps telling me what he did when he played. I don't think I can be that good. What should I do?

First, I suspect that your dad spent years working on his game, just as you will. Believe me: It is virtually impossible to predict how well you will play five years from now. I suggest that you sit down with your dad and talk at length about when he started playing, about how he learned to throw, hit, catch, and run. You may jog his memory a little bit, and a reminder of just how difficult baseball is to learn will be very helpful, not only for him but for you. Remembering his own first years in the sport, he may decide to work with you on basic skills. Things will work out well for both of you. You will be better and he will again appreciate how difficult it is to play the game.

BRIAN JORDAN
Outfielder, Atlanta Braves

★ Three years with Atlanta Braves
★ Eight years in professional baseball

I started playing baseball at eight years old. Actually, I played baseball, basketball, and football all the way through high school, and played both baseball and football in college at the University of Richmond.

But even when playing other sports growing up, I always seemed to do better in baseball. I played varsity baseball as freshman in high school, which was not often done at my school. So I knew early on that baseball was going to be my dominant sport.

I was always an infielder growing up. In fact, I was drafted by Cleveland out of high school as a shortstop/second baseman. But I went to college and began to play outfield, and I've been in the outfield ever since.

My dad was probably the most influential person in my younger days as a baseball player. He was always giving me tips. But both my parents were always very supportive. And my older brother and sister, who are twins, were also great athletes. I came from a very athletic family.

I always had fun in youth baseball, and, eventually, I learned how to be a good sport. That was a very tough lesson for me because I always wanted to win, to dominate, to be the best player. My children are the same way; they really hate to lose. They play to win, which is good, but you have to learn that you don't win all the time.

The other thing I learned – and hope my kids are learning – is to never give up. Use all the talent you've got and never fall short in effort.

My advice to parents is to do everything you can to support your children in sports. Get your kids out there and get them involved. It's such a great place for them to be.

When it comes to selecting the right program for your kids, I suggest you look for one that has clinics. I think it's very important for kids to learn to play the game correctly. Not only will they get better faster, but they will have more fun.

I would advise coaches to always be patient and positive. I had a few yellers and screamers coaching me when I was young, and even though they were good teachers, the yelling doesn't help. It's very important for these kids to develop positive self-esteem. Along these same lines, coaches should definitely spend time with *all* the kids, not just the best athletes.

I think coaches should push when it's needed and stay after their players to get better. But you've got to allow them to grow up in sport. You've got to teach them that, ultimately, they have responsibility.

Probably the most important thing coaches can teach kids is that if you always give your best effort, you win. You can take that success away with you, regardless of the score on the scoreboard.

One other thing I'd tell coaches is that we're starting the All-Star thing way too early. Probably age 12 or 13 is about the right time. But it's not good for the younger players. When they see others make the All-Star team and they're left off, they may quit the sport. It can be a detriment to the development of their self-esteem, and youth baseball should be all about building up self-esteem.

How should coaches deal with the problem of unruly parents? Here's what I would do. I'd begin by calling a meeting with all the parents. I'd keep it positive, but I'd tell them how it's going to be.

⦿ The kids are there to have fun.

⦿ They're all going to play.

⦿ They're all going to learn how to play the game.

⦿ We're not going to be so serious.

And I would ask the parents to please not do things to let the kids down. Please don't embarrass the kids.

As parents, I would tell them, you should be

there to watch the kids, and to support them every day. This sport is about the kids, not about the coach and not about the parents.

9. How do professional players get so good?

There are many reasons, and of course it varies from player to player, but here are a few keys:

● They have always played the game with enthusiasm.

● They love the game.

● They had good instruction when they were young and learned the correct mechanics.

● They know how to deal with winning and how to deal with losing.

● They value fitness and they work hard during the off-season to stay in shape both physically and mentally.

The important thing to remember, though, is that when they started to play baseball, they were not any better than you.

10. My parents don't seem to like baseball. They won't come to my games. How can I get them there?

It may not be that they don't like the game. It may be just a matter of their priorities. Sit and talk with your parents about what you are learning at practice. Ask them to play with you in the yard, throwing and catching. Then maybe they'll want to come and watch what you have been working on together. Parents too often see their work as their way of supporting you. You may have to remind them that you need other kinds of support as well. You may need to remind them that taking an interest in your activities – that being with you – is the kind of support that really means something.

Conclusion

Baseball is such a wonderful game – so exciting, so challenging, and so much fun. Here's what I suggest we do: let's give it back to the kids – a gift from the heart, with no obligation. They don't have to be great at it. They don't have to give us parents and coaches something to brag about. They don't have to take on the burden of our own dreams and hopes. They don't have to earn a college scholarship. They don't have to go pro. All they have to do is enjoy it.

When the weather warms and the grass greens up, a lot of kids want to play baseball.

I say, "Let 'em play."